Know Your Children As They Are

A Book For Parents

Caleb Gattegno

Educational Solutions Worldwide Inc.

First published in the United States of America in 1988. Reprinted in 2010.

Copyright © 1988-2010 Educational Solutions Worldwide Inc.
Author: Caleb Gattegno
All rights reserved
ISBN 978-0-87825-191-9

Educational Solutions Worldwide Inc.
2nd Floor 99 University Place, New York, N.Y. 10003-4555
www.EducationalSolutions.com

Table of Contents

Preface 1

Part I: From Conception to Elementary School 7

    Introduction: A Baby is a Learning System 9

    1 Prenatal Preparation: The Work of the Embryo 13

    2 Entering The World: Meeting the Environment 21

        Why do Babies Cry? 25

        What is Sleep? 27

        Serene Sleep, Smiling Health, Emotions 29

    3 Processing Energy: Learning to Use the Senses 33

    4 Temporal Hierarchies: Why Babies do one Thing Rather Than Another 41

        Living in Time 45

        The Tools of Synthesis and Analysis, and of Intuition 48

        The Adventures of Babies 50

        The Changing World and the Changing Self 53

    5 Talking: How Babies Master Sound Making 57

    6 Speaking: How Babies Master Language 69

    7 Learning Other Things: Children Investigating Their Universe 85

    8 The Love that Babies and Young Children Need 99

Part II: Of Boys and Girls 111

Introduction 113

9 Perception at the Service of Action: Marbles and Hopscotch 115

10 Action at the Service of Perception: Why Children Draw 123

11 Imagery, Virtuality, Symbolism: Extending the World of Action 129

12 Finesse and Balance: Jump Rope and Other Games of Energy 137

13 Filling the World with Dynamics 145

14 Games: Their Phases, Purposes, and Opportunities 151

15 Drawings: Self—Knowledge and the Power of Sight 161

16 Partnerships: The Necessary Selfishness of Children 167

17 Equity and Morality: The Ethic of Action 175

18 Interest and Lack of Interest 181

19 Before Adolescence: On the Threshold of a New World 185

Part III: Spotlights on Adolescence 193

Introduction: What is Adolescence? 195

20 The Discovery of Friendship 199

21 The Discovery of Religion 203

22 The Discovery of Thought 207

23 The Adolescent and Love 215

Further Readings 221

Preface

Parents love their children, but do they understand them?

For the most part, they don't. And they don't because the task is huge, and science has still to recognize the existence of the task and to work on it.

This book is a contribution to making the general public aware that children can be understood if grown-ups do what is required — that is, try to make sense of what children do with their time to change it into experience.

What children do varies of course with their ages. The different tasks of different periods is what we shall explore in this three-part book. The first part focuses on babies, the second part on young children, the third part on adolescents.

As adults, we have all gone through these three phases of life and have moved on to other fields of interest. In doing so, we have mostly lost contact with the process of living the earlier stages and have forgotten the real meaning of these years.

Today, however, we can regain and maintain the contact with our own past, not by remembering this or that event but by becoming aware of the dynamics inherent in acts of living. This is a new grown-up occupation, and it goes with being a parent and needing to know what parenthood entails. Uncovering the dynamics of the early years of life is the aim of this book.

There are no "shoulds" in this book. But one might be urged in this preface.

Consider the following. Procreation is instinctual in animals. Humans, however, have sharply separated the capacity to have offspring, which follows the advent of puberty, from the capacity to get married or raise a family, activities that are social and, today, economic. This separation is one clear sign that instinct plays no part in the structuring of human life. Instead, as we shall see more clearly in the pages that follow, we structure our lives by engaging for long periods in exploring systematically what we need to know to forge ahead.

I call these periods "temporal hierarchies." In the present we live intensely what our passion to know presents us with, and we do this so that we constantly master more of ourselves and our environment. We shift to new fields of experience once we have mastered previous fields. There is thus an ordering in our experience, a hierarchy that exists in time, a temporal hierarchy.

Why does this matter to us as parents? Temporal hierarchies apply to all of us, and when we become parents, we must activate in ourselves the outlook that recognizes such processes.

It is from this perspective that we need to look at our children — from where they are and what they have to do. Now, children cannot do this for us. This task is our obligation as parents. Parents <u>can</u> see the reality of their evolving children. As the children's spontaneous fields of study change, so the children change, and parents too must change. We go against reality if we unchangingly consider our children as <u>our</u> children. If that were the whole truth, there would be no change. Since it is not the whole truth, we must change so that we may gain access to what we ourselves had to do at the age of our children to gain the experience we gained.

Parents can ask themselves: "Do I have a clear idea of what there is to be learned at the level of perception? Or at the level of action? Or about one's inner life?" As we shall see, perception is the area that engages babies and young children, action is the area that engages older children, the inner life is the area that engages adolescents. If, to these questions, parents answer "No" or "Only slightly" — which is usually the case — then the truth is we are blind to the needs of our children, just as our own parents were blind to our needs as children.

In this book we have attempted to gather the practical essentials of what we have learned in our long examination of children, from babies to adolescents, as they engage in those tasks of learning that change their time into experience.

For those who want to explore in more detail this way of thinking about children — which essentially is a way of thinking about human experience — one of the texts from which selections were drawn for this volume can be obtained from Education Solutions, 95 University Place, New York, NY 10003-4555: <u>In the Beginning There Were No Words: The Universe of Babies</u>.

Readers will soon find that the three parts of this work are of different lengths, although the duration of the growing phase that they refer to is approximately the same. The reasons for these discrepancies are many. We note the following:

1. There are very few reliable works on very early childhood, and therefore there is a greater need to know more about it, and to recognize particularly that these very important years for all of us, if well understood, will inspire changes in education in the home and in child-care centers that can have tremendous consequences in the future.

2. Once the instruments of study for the early years have been found reliable and fruitful, they will be used for the study of later years and do not need to be presented again.

3. As we grow up and change the stress on what occupies us, the descriptions of our exchanges of time for experience can become more abstract in order to be more comprehensive. This increased abstraction will be seen in the alteration of the style from part to part.

4. It also seems right that the variety of different challenges examined in each part impose their separate requirements on the method of discourse. Had there been one way of telling all the stories in this examination of growing up, it might have been

adopted, but I know of none. Therefore, I do not apologize for the very different climate found in the three parts of this work. But I feel the need to warn readers who may prefer a uniform treatment of all these early years, that this will not be the case here.

I would also tell readers who are parents that the allocation of less space in this book to the phase of adolescence must not be translated into believing that it has less importance than the previous two phases. On the contrary, we must meet each phase at the moment it is most important for our children and meet it in the way that they do, and not relativize what are absolutes for our children. Early childhood is lost in our past, but the work of adolescence has a greater impact on our relationships to our parents and may take many years to be put right, sometimes twenty years, as so many of us have found. Therefore, it is advisable for parents to become much more sensitive than perhaps they have been to what their adolescent children must do for themselves and with themselves.

It remains for me here to thank Harris Dienstfrey for his work of editing and Diana Werbel for her typing of the text that became this book.

Caleb Gattegno
Winter 1988

Part I

From Conception to Elementary School

Introduction:
A Baby is a Learning System

When I was born, I must have looked as if I only knew a few things - sleeping, eating, crying and evacuating.

This is what outsiders could say and probably did say because appearances dictated these conclusions.

But little did my parents know that I was working hard to learn to do all those new things I had never done before.

Parents indeed do not know what they themselves did with their time as children, nor what their children are doing with their time. Parents are too busy doing what they need to do for themselves and their charges, including the newly born child, to watch for the reality behind the appearances and to understand the use of time by babies.

Part I
From Conception to Elementary School

In this book we shall ask ourselves some hard questions about the activities of babies, and if we can answer them in an acceptable manner, we shall perhaps know something about our own remotest past.

Because we want to understand babies who have neither been studied seriously enough nor known intimately enough, we must impose a new discipline on ourselves.

The discipline consists of examining whether we are really in contact with the challenge we seek to understand.

Here is an exercise to indicate in precise terms what we mean. Many people say, "Children learn to speak by imitation," and are convinced it is true. But if they really want to know whether it is true, they should ask themselves what they mean by imitation. Do they mean that a baby <u>sees</u> what a speaker does with his throat or tongue and then reproduces these actions? Or do they mean that if the ability to do these things were known to a child, it would be easy for him or her to do what others do — although in fact the child only <u>hears</u> people in the environment speaking?

Neither alternative is imitation as it is generally understood by those who use the word.

No one can learn to speak by imitation simply because we hear with our ears and speak with our vocal system. The one system is reached by impacts from the environment and the other is a totally voluntary system. In addition, we each speak with our own voice while hearing the voices of <u>others</u>. So how can there have been imitation?

In this book, one of the tools for understanding ourselves as babies is to recognize the existence of a continuing property of the self, one which is known by everyone at all stages in life — <u>self-awareness</u>. If I know at this moment what I want to write down but do not know in the same way how I hold and guide the instrument for writing, there was still a time when I had to conquer the skill of writing and be totally absorbed in it to achieve its mastery. Both activities are the result of self-awareness.

In a similar way, my not knowing <u>now</u> what I did to reach so thorough a knowledge of my skin that I can coordinate the acts needed to chase or crush an insect creating a sensation on my neck or back does not preclude that I did work consciously to become aware of how to interpret messages before entering into an action. The development of the somatic self is accompanied by a process of awareness.

However reluctant readers may be to adopt the assumption that <u>somatic consciousness</u> has been as vivid and as well known to the self as social or intellectual consciousness is today, I suggest that they entertain it for a while in order to find out what help it provides in understanding babies (or for that matter any age and any condition).

One feature of the new instrument of self-awareness is that it puts the self of each of us in the most intimate contact with the forms usually studied from the outside, and places consciousness in active and searching contact with all that the self does. Because consciousness is the key to change — all change — the concept of self-awareness makes it possible to use one and the same language at the somatic, mental, and spiritual levels.

In the following discussion on the work of babies, we shall conceive of each person — each baby — as a learning system that does not need to be motivated externally in order to acknowledge perceptions and become engaged in actions. This learning system contains its own dynamic. It is also a learning system that is changed by learning and that therefore has the capacity to encounter new perceptions and become involved in new actions, which in turn affect and change the system.

1 Prenatal Preparation: The Work of the Embryo

It takes only a few days or weeks for parents to know whether a fertilized ovule is growing into a future baby. The knowledge comes from the changes in the mother's condition which signal that the environment in which the baby will grow is adapting to the baby's needs.

Embryologists have studied a number of aspects of this growth, and any biology book will state how the egg, made of the fusion of an ovule with a spermatozoid, starts and pursues a dual process of subdivision and growth that leads to the specialized tissues and then to organs. Molecular biologists have asked deeper questions and have wanted to understand how each moment of growth can be described in chemical terms, which can then be ascertained by chemical tests.

But the explanatory schemas offered by scientists are confused. On the one hand, scientists acknowledge that each individual organism must make itself from material that is less complex than itself and is obtainable from the environment. On the other, they maintain that the complex process of synthesis must be given in advance, in the individual as it were, so as to produce an individual of a particular species. The various blue-prints are said to be passed on from generation to generation as inscriptions on the hereditary stuff called DNA and on the items called genes that affect each particular state.

For our purpose here, it is perhaps permissible to by-pass a schema that uses a language only specialists understand. In more everyday terms, we can say that the unborn baby of any species receives from the environment, that is, from the mother, the ingredients that the blood of the mother brings the embryo. This blood, however much it is affected by the reaction of the mother's organism to the semi-foreign body hooked onto the wall of her uterus, is the same as the blood that she uses in her own cells. Her cells are already completed and are serviced in certain ways by the content of the blood. But the embryo's cells must be synthesized by the embryo itself out of both the existing substances that form its present somatic stage and the substances that are in the mother's blood. What if this blood is deficient in some substance? The embryo must either produce it or live with the consequence of its absence, which means not being able to do some jobs that other specimens do normally. Similarly, if the mother's blood carries some chemicals not needed for the pursuit of the embryo's development, the embryo must either filter them out and protect itself from them or suffer the consequences of having to integrate unnecessary elements.

It is clear that the relationship between a mother and her embryo is not a simple one, or a perfectly predictable one. It is also a relationship that offers the possibility of leading to unique individuals. In fact, <u>no two living organisms can be identical</u>.

In the case of human beings, whose diets may differ considerably, the dependence of the embryo on the content of the mother's blood introduces a variable that may radically change one offspring from the next. If the synthesis of chemicals that form the contents of the cells in the various tissues is simultaneously conditioned by the raw material available and by the possibility of hosting some chemical reactions but not others, we can see that each individual works to form his or her own chemical self. For this reason, we will not talk as if all the processes were governed by "natural laws." Such views are not in touch with the realities faced by the embryo.

People who speak of "the embryo" are appealing to a metaphysical entity. They write: "The embryo develops as instructed by a ready-made program conditioned by the DNA of the first cell." But this can be a legitimate statement only for someone describing outside appearances.

Every embryo is indeed endowed with a program that continues a species. But every embryo must also synthesize itself out of material which it does not control and which may be deficient or redundant in the chemicals required. Though it is possible to offer a description of embryonic development that uses the plausible language of blueprints, of reactions and chemicals, it is also possible to develop an alternative language that is more responsive to the embryo's work at the prenatal level and that reveals the compatibility of this work with the self-determination of the individual at later stages.

Consider the cell's dual movement of growth and subdivision, each then following the other, until tissues are formed. This is followed by another dual movement out of which the organs (or functional tissues) are constituted and then by another which develops specific functionings. We shall find this dual movement of elaboration and utilization all through life, in the acquisition of skills in particular.

If in later life I find I have criteria that tell me to continue the elaboration of part of myself (and the functionings that belong to it) rather than simply to utilize it, I can also see that the jobs to be done in utero obey the same requirements. However little was given to me in the egg, it nonetheless was sufficient to make me capable of using this little to give myself a form that remains with me as an intrinsic part of myself — as indeed does any skill developed during this period.

From outside we all look as if we were enclosed in our individual, self-contained "bags," of which our skin is a token, and that we consist of what normally is perceived to be the contents of the bag. When some people found muscles and bones in each bag, they provided a model of man that could move around. As other people found lungs and a heart, the model became more complex, and respiration and circulation were added to it, with their respective functions of oxygenating the blood and the combustion of food stuffs in the cells (to produce the energy to maintain the body's temperature and to cope with locomotion). Then the digestive tract, as the supplier of broken-down chemicals for both storage and the elimination of waste, was added. Others discovered the nervous system and its refined sensitivities. Others found hormones and the functions of glands, and others vitamins and enzymes as the catalysts of the many chemical reactions performed continuously by all organisms. Still others found that the psyche acts on the functions and organs to transform them, and so the psyche was added to the arsenal of instruments for understanding man.

Now, the movement of these discoveries — we might call them "uncoverings" — was clearly away from immediate appearances towards less and less obvious elements, complicating indefinitely the model of ourselves we had to carry with us if we wanted to understand ourselves.

Clearly, we do not acquire enzymes or hormones as we grow older or only after a certain stage of development. Not only are they there from the start, but much of what molecular biologists added to our knowledge of man (and animals) is the outcome of the recognition that the subtle activities of enzymes are indispensable to the production in the embryo of the various proteins that will specialize the cells into tissues and organs. Some scientists have tended to locate in the egg all the potential for growth that other scientists have shifted to the brain. But since the egg precedes the constitution of the tissues which will become the brain, the material that is in the egg conditions the sort of brain and the kind of functionings that are possible.

These few sentences begin to evoke the enormous complexity of the work that is performed <u>in utero</u>.

As a developing organism, there are functions not asked of me (such as speaking a language) and others that I cannot postpone (such as structuring my organs). Hence, I shall not give any time to what is irrelevant and give all my attention to the task on hand — in the sense that I give my attention to the task of writing this, closing myself to all distractions by using my consciousness in a pinpointed way (within the synthesis of years of somatic awareness) so as to hold the pen and force it to design these and no other words.

<u>All my attention</u>, at the level of the embryo, means that there is an alternation of intense conscious elaboration followed by a consolidation of the elaborated form, which then becomes a kind of "automatism" that no longer needs all one's attention. Instead, the elaborated form now needs only as little consciousness as is required to survey it and to signal any possible dysfunction in it to the much larger portion of consciousness that has been freed from the task of elaboration. This whole elaboration and consolidation is followed by a shift towards using the elaborated form for new tasks that now gather all one's attention to produce the next "automatism," which again maintains itself with an absolute minimum of consciousness, thereby freeing the self to meet more complex tasks with the new elaborated form that has become available. And so on.

1 Prenatal Preparation: The Work of the Embryo

Man begins with one single cell, like amoebae or bacteria, because life can take that form, as proved by the existence of the single-cell organisms. As a single cell it is not a full being, but since the cell has the capabilities (not yet fully understood in the case of multicellular organisms) that permit it to gather chemicals to maintain life, the living egg begins a human life at the somatic level and begins to transform itself. In every one of us, the functions of the egg are still alive, as are all their transformations.

The enormous jobs of the human embryo — of making proteins by combining the amino acids brought by the flow of mother's blood with both the enzymes already in the egg and those in the blood, of alternating the fine controls that produce a stoppage of growth at precise moments and then start a subdivision followed by new growth, of letting some chemicals then take over that control — all this is the conscious life of the embryo. No part of the soma, which from outside is called a "body," is formed without the active presence of consciousness manifesting itself at every moment as an extremely sensitive chemist, extremely knowledgeable about what is required and how to achieve it with the supply of chemicals from the sources of the mother's blood and the egg.

2 Entering the World: Meeting the Environment

Once the baby is born, observing it is obviously easier, and we can pick up many facts that will help us understand what babies do with themselves in the first few weeks of life. According to popular wisdom, babies during this period sleep most of the day, cry when they wake up, eat and evacuate, and seem not to have any other concerns. But this view considers no more than surface appearances.

Since the environment changes radically at one's birth, the newly born baby now has a number of new functions thrust upon him. He must take air through his lungs and oxidize his blood himself. Because his food was formerly processed by his mother and sent to his system through the umbilical cord, now that the cord is cut, he must take in his own food through his mouth and process it to the levels his functioning organs are used to. He must learn how to do with his digestive tract what his mother unconsciously has done for him until now.

Part I
From Conception to Elementary School

In the womb the embryo was held by a cushion of liquid, and now the baby lies on the kind of bed his culture supplies for babies: soft or hard, it is certainly harder than the womb.

He will be covered and dressed according to the requirements adults impose, and he has to learn to adjust to these demands.

He did not have to inhale until now, and now his nose may have to cope with particles that affect his skin and produce new behaviors (responses to the environment), which have to be known before they can be done adequately.

The unsophisticated belief that all this is acquired by "instinct" is certainly out of place in understanding the newly born baby.

If we know that the vigilant self of the baby that did so much prenatal work, is still vigilant and ready to use what it is and what it has to adjust to its new challenges, there will be no need for a miraculous entity like instinct to explain what babies do with themselves after birth.

Since the embryo in the womb has no need to process pressures from the outside, its sense organs are made of bunched-up nerve fibers that can transmit only an overall impact to the centers. For a time after birth, consciousness is still, so to say, refused to these bunched-up nerves. However, other nerves are active — in particular those that command the peristaltic movements of the digestive tract whenever the ingested food touches it.

The lips must learn to hold on to the nipple. Then the muscles of the mouth must pump liquid with the lips, and while the liquid is in the mouth, the tongue must hold the liquid so that the epiglottis closes the opening of the trachea (with the vocal cords) and the uvula closes the passage to the nose. Then the tongue must bend to deliver the liquid to the esophagus. All these new demands <u>must be learned</u> and learned quickly and well, for the burning of reserves will create an imbalance requiring replenishment.

Mother's milk is mainly water to begin with, and so the rest of the digestive tract will not have much to do at this time. After a few meals the baby masters sucking, swallowing, and the coordination of the demands of breathing and swallowing. Because pumping is voluntary and because the self can interpret the impacts on both the various parts of the mouth and the functioning of these parts, an alert consciousness handles the matter usually without hitches and, indeed, gives the impression of an innate predetermined and inherited behavior. But we soon see the limits of this "instinctive" attack as we consider the new demands from life.

Consciousness is required to learn to avoid taking air into the digestive tube when swallowing one's food. For months the newly born baby struggles with learning this task. Adults may still have a problem with it, and some cultures allow belching as an acceptable way of restoring the separation of eating from breathing.

As the days go by and the food becomes more consistent, the different phases of digestion need to be practiced.

Saliva is produced in the mouth in quantities not yet under control. In the stomach the gastric juices are mixed with the salivated food, and reflexes are triggered by the presence of matter and its contact with the glands in the walls. The various glands in the digestive tube begin to learn to respond to the varying composition of the mother's milk that partially replace the substances drawn from the mother's blood. Some of the reserves in the liver, the spleen, and the marrow are called in while the digestive functions are made to work properly.

The waste from the cells, instead of being directed to the umbilical cord, must now go to the bladder and the large intestine, and there, too, there are new functions to learn. Since there is normally no continuous evacuation, we must conclude that a certain degree of habituation to the accumulation of waste takes place quite early. The sphincters are voluntary muscles, and they are closed and opened at will. In the beginning of life in the world, it is entirely an inner decision of the baby that keeps them closed or open. Later this decision will be coordinated with other considerations and lead to the abandoning of diapers.

The baby who takes in what his mother gives him from her breasts or from bottles has no control any more on what he filters or accepts. He learns to throw up, he develops diarrhea or constipation to cope with the unknown chemical composition of his food when it does not agree with him. He may refuse to eat when his sensors recognize some chemicals that are not acceptable to his state. Even the care of "nature" that is at work in the metabolism of the mother cannot altogether ensure that the milk offered the baby will not trigger rejection by him in one form or the other.

Thus, there is plenty to learn during the first few weeks. Moreover, during that time, the baby is intensely engaged in new vital jobs that have just come his way. We will consider two of them: crying and sleeping.

Why do Babies Cry?

Crying is a form of activity all babies use as soon as they are born. It comes about because of what is available to them from their previous stage. It is not aimed at the environment, though the people in it consider it a call for help. But the baby is not aware that help exists. Crying originally comes to him as a form of activity compatible with his state, and only later will it be used as a tool to relate to people in the way they expect.

Many parents have been at a loss to understand why their baby cries so much. Some babies do not indulge in crying. Some do not cry at all for a long time, and parents may consider them to be subnormal. The vast majority of babies do cry. Some cry for a certain duration at the same hour every day for some months for no reason understandable to anyone.

Let us first look at crying as originating in the baby and afterwards link it with the other forms originating in the environment.

When air passes through the larynx, the voluntary vocal cords can control its emergence from the (voluntary) mouth. The flow of air touching the walls of the inner cavity of the mouth (palate, tongue, cheeks, uvula) and of the nostrils, is recognized by its impacts there. Babies, already conscious of somatic changes, engage themselves in the thorough study of these impacts and their range of variation. Crying, for the baby, is the pursuit of this study.

It is well known that in a nursery babies just a few hours after birth join other babies in a crying chorus, giving the impression that they hear and imitate sounds from the start. Because the baby has already mastered before birth all that is required in order to know from the inside what crying is, and because the auditory nerve (even as a bunched-up set of fibers) can take to a baby's consciousness the impact of other babies crying, any baby who is not deaf will interpret at once that other people are doing what he can do, and he proves it by doing it.

Now, since only the baby knows when his system is short of energy or when a muscle is tensed or a tendon is twisted or when poison is at work in his tract, and since he can simultaneously use his breathing and his vocal cords, we find that the circumstances that demand casual but necessary attention put him into contact with the environment through the only open channel available to him: his throat. Hence, once again, babies cry because they can and not to call for help. Cries express the awareness that one is forced to stop doing a job and cannot solve on one's own the problem with which one is faced.

That cries soon become a code between the learning baby and the environment should not obscure the fact that awareness is present in such crying too, and present in its own form and for its own purposes. Mothers, like their babies, know that there are many kinds of crying and that each has components indicating a special awareness of what the baby is engaged in.

The intensity, duration, and pitch all convey that the child's self is either in contact with a pain of one kind or another, or is simply playing at crying in order to learn about noise production and the modulation of sounds.

Crying, both when it is for the baby himself and when it is a form of communication, serves to alert babies to the possibilities of conscious investigation in the realm of sound. We shall see later to what good use young children put this apprenticeship to the task of talking and speaking.

What is Sleep?

As the baby becomes involved in the vital new jobs of mastering such tasks as eating, breathing, and evacuating, he withdraws his consciousness from his hearing and leads a solitary life of his own. His chemical sense guides him to his source of food, and he takes in what restores his chemical equilibrium. When this is achieved and he stops eating, he goes back to his work, and then looks to be asleep.

To be asleep is two things in one. For the outsider, it is a withdrawal from the world; for the sleeper, it is the return to what he knows best and has lived with most intimately.

Since we relate best to ourselves when asleep, and relate to others only when awake, here again there are many sources of confusion in trying to understand reality according to whether we stress the inner or the outer life.

Withdrawal into our own bag is to take ourselves to our own domain where knowledge and knowing reign. There we have only ourselves to contend with, and we know freedom because of the mastery we have of our functionings and because of our awareness of the dynamics of our energy.

This view of sleep makes much more sense than the notion that sleep serves the need to recuperate or that it is a mysterious process of wasting the time we could use for living. In particular, the capacity for solving problems that accompanies some of our nights of sleep is seen here as the outcome of the exercise of our freedom in a universe where the self reigns.

Now, let us consider a variety of elements observable in babies at this time.

Serene Sleep, Smiling Health, Emotions

The baby at this stage generally looks serene in sleep. Instrumental study of the state of his muscle tone shows a harmonious curve, as if the baby was imperturbable.

Because the sense organs have not yet been used to structure the mental energy that will soon activate them (this process will be examined in the next chapter), there are no images in the bag besides the body-image. The baby therefore does not dream.

The changes that are visible from outside on the skin of the baby are the outcome of the impact of energy changes on the muscle tone all over his body. These changes accompany development of the vital functionings now being studied and mastered. When, for example, the flow of food in the tract is smooth, either no external change is visible or an elusive wave runs over the surface of the soma and forms around the lips and the cheeks what everyone calls a smile. A newly born baby can only "smile at the angels," for he is unaware of people in his neighborhood.

Any breakdown, small or large, in the new functionings can have considerable repercussions in the soma and is often accompanied by a great expenditure of energy through crying. Because the self is so close to its structure and its functionings, each baby is his own best physician. For example, the true meaning of the state of falling into a coma is the need for a total withdrawal of the self's energies so as to enable it to handle an aggression — in the form, say, of a poison or a foreign body.

Babies in their very early days cure themselves and may go through diseases with no one suspecting the need for help.

It has often been said that newly born babies are born immune to a number of diseases, including the common cold. It seems more appropriate to say that the architect, the builder, the maintenance agent of the soma are so close to the structure and the functionings that any disturbance is caught as soon as it starts and is taken care of at once. As consciousness moves towards other concerns, external help becomes necessary when illnesses occur. In the very young baby, health is the normal state, even when congenital defects exist. Most of these defects will become felt only when some functions emerge other than those essential for survival. (Death in early childhood may express an inadequacy of the somatic construction, but many deformed and handicapped children do survive.)

In the bag alongside the objectified energy — expressed in structures and functionings — there is free energy which the self can distribute, reserve, or displace at will. When energy is mobilized but not objectified it gains a temporary form. We shall call <u>emotions</u> the "coagulation" of energy that the self recognizes within itself and that it can recuperate and reallocate.

Young babies already know this dynamic of energy, and they use it very early in response or reaction to some aspects of the environment. They get involved for a very short time in some connection with people or with things but abruptly go back to their main "preoccupation." Indeed, if the enormous content of the environment were attractive to children of that age, it would exhaust all their energy, however much there is. Hence, babies on their own choose to "lend" rather than give their attention, and they produce temporary inner impacts — emotions — that confirm to themselves that the dynamics of the energy in their bag is directed by their consciousness.

Let us sum up the content of this chapter. We have followed the entry into our world of a being who knew the universe of his bag thoroughly, and we have found how he manages to relate creatively to new demands. The detailed descriptions of the new performances make us know babies as they need to be known — as learners and not as reflex mechanisms triggered by conditionings.

3 Processing Energy:
Learning to use the Senses

Parents say that their babies are "seeing" if the babies follow a moving finger or a moving light with their eyes. They say that babies are "hearing" if they turn their head when dad or someone else snaps his fingers on one side and then the other. Parents dispute among themselves about their children's use of sense organs, because there is so often the appearance of perception in children but not the expected consistency of perception.

We have already noticed that newly born babies in hospital nurseries display the phenomenon of contagious crying, an aural phenomenon. They can also open their eyes, that is, order their eyelids to separate and remain in that state for a while. These appearances seem to indicate a self active at the level of perception. But the baby knows better. When all his attention is required by studies which are essential for survival, he will not engage in activities that are less vital at the time.

Pediatricians tell parents that for a few weeks after birth babies are insensitive to pain. Doctors perform operations like circumcision and the opening of the canals in the lachrymal glands without anesthetics. Anatomy books tell of a phenomenon called the "myelinization of the sensory nerves" which takes place a few weeks after birth and is presumably the point when babies become open to pain.

When myelinization occurs, which may be 4 to 6 weeks after birth, a sheath of fat is produced to surround each nerve fiber and insulate it from the other fibers, rather like the wires in a telegraph cable. Doctors say that only after this has happened can sensations reach the centers that register impacts and cause pain to be felt. This is not quite what closer observers can see. The facial expressions of babies operated upon without anesthetics during the first week after birth, and the crying of those babies, indicate that they note the aggression and "resent" it. But since they cope immediately with the somatic disturbance and are masters at coping with events at that level, they generally start the healing process at once and apply their consciousness so intensively to that job that little attention is left for unknown functions such as impressing the environment. If some complication results, say from infection or the clumsiness of the "surgeon," it is the deviation of energy from the known to the unknown that generates the traumatism and its expressions. Babies are at home with the soma that they made during the preceding months and know exactly what to do to cope with the events that make sense within that awareness. But as in the rest of life, they will be uncertain when forced to consider what is transcendental to them at the moment. They must then fall back upon guesswork as a response to the impact. If they are lucky, their struggle will be victorious; if not, a scar may remain in the bag from then on.

The myelinization of the sensory nerves brings about an important change, however. Since the process takes a few days, the transformation of the self through the experience is gradual, and babies learn to place their consciousness upon those inner changes that result from the arrival of outside energy through the opened channels of their senses. One day, a few days after myelinization begins, babies seem to be seeing and hearing. For babies themselves, the work of receiving the impact of the world started with their capacity to analyze a mental operation accompanying the somatic transformation of each sensory nerve. With myelinization, the many thousands of nerve fibers, each associated at one end with a sense organ and at the other with a cell in the brain, are now capable of transforming impacts into inputs because they bring additional energy to the baby's soma. The processing of such energy is the story of how the baby <u>learns</u> to use his senses.

The anatomical eye is made before birth. Seeing is no more the immediate result of opening one's eyes than digestion is the consequence of receiving food. There is much to learn in seeing and in the other sensory functions. In fact, it takes years of subtle and continuous work to reach a high level of seeing, hearing, and feeling, because sensory functions relate each individual to a universe that is in flux and that therefore is never completely knowable.

Because eyes, ears and skin offer consciousness different ways of receiving outside energy, new ways of knowing emerge which in turn make the self aware of itself in a multitude of different ways. This multiple self-awareness accounts for the uniqueness of the individual. What we do with ourselves in the total environment makes us into the persons we are. But what we are is never finished because our continuing encounter with other persons shows us ways of being that were open to us but which we have not actualized in our own lives, and through such encounters we can change.

Once the sensory organs come into active use, the individual self engages more and more of itself in becoming aware of what can be done with the further instruments available to it and with the further instruments that they in turn produce.

Consider the eyes.

Our eyes are made of parts that can be described anatomically, optically, mechanically, and physiologically. All have their role in the function of seeing. The eyeballs are moved in their sockets by small muscles attached to the bones and to the eyeball. These muscles are voluntary, linked to the brain by nerves that obey orders from the will. Babies have to learn to instruct these muscles to do what their self wills. At birth eye movements are free to be educated by the self engaged in seeing, and most children spend many hours over the years attempting to take the eye muscles to the point that they know is possible if they have' seen someone in their environment do it.

Further, although most of us are born with the capacity to "open" our eyes, once the optical system is open to the world, it can become the object of attention when light reaches it, bringing to the eye, and therefore the self, a new input of energy. The baby responds to this impact when it is ready.

The opening to the optical eye is made of a circular muscle that acts like a diaphragm in a camera, controlling the number of photons allowed in. For most of us its opening and closing is regulated by the amount of light reaching the eye. Such regulation is one of the automatisms organized by the self by delegating decisions to a special somatic compact.

But the act of focusing is also voluntary. The sources of light are scattered all over space, and we need to interpret all the time the impacts of photons on the retina. In order to know the content of space, we have to relate consciously to the alterations that occur in our soma from the state of the iris, the state of the lens, the optic fibers that have been activated, the part of the retina that is struck by photons, and the individual and collective quality of the photons.

If we compare the naive view that eyes in and of themselves are made for seeing against the enormous tasks we really have to engage in in order to use the eyes to learn to see, the place of consciousness becomes evident. As a baby everyone of us needs to become aware of what the act of seeing involves so that we can achieve the automatization that leaves us free for the other tasks involving seeing. For weeks each of us relates the energy of more and more photons to affect special areas of the brain and to add to the somatic energy available to us.

In the developments that follow, we can find the origin of dreaming, the imagination, and the power to symbolize.

A "film" of environmental light-changes can be assembled every day by the baby from material that he owns. When he is asleep, the energy in the "film" is available to the control of a consciousness capable of perceiving identities, similarities, differences, durations — characteristics that are connected with the working instruments already available in his bag. This dialogue of the self in sleep is the process that makes the eye into an "image factory." The eye, instead of receiving photons now from outside, is made the judge (somatically) of the energy alterations that the will produces by pouring energy into the cells to bring about the effects caused by the photons from the environment. The self in the soma, the sleeping self to the observer, is very busy educating the eye to evoke images at will — that is, to comprehend what it is seeing.

Once visual images gain an existence of their own as semi-free energy in the bag, their life, mainly in the sleeping state, gains the autonomy to make dreams, and makes dreaming a new power of the self. In dreams the constraints of "reality" are no longer compulsory. New realities can be manufactured, and the realm of the imagination is opened. Imagination becomes more and more a test of one's humanity because it is an expression of freedom.

The power to symbolize is also gained in this development, for once images gain their own existence the self knows both the reality of things and the reality of knowing <u>about</u> things. As the shift from one to the other becomes easier, better equipped, more frequent, the self finds for itself the endowment that comes from living with things, among things, and also next to them, outside them. The fact that evocation can replace actuality for some purposes is the source of symbolism as a power. From this power many others result during the journey through life.

The example of sight alone shows us how much babies have to learn after they have assured their survival outside the mother's womb. Hearing and feeling present comparable challenges. We shall not consider them here, except to say that almost all babies master them, one more sign of their powerful capabilities and their remarkable achievements.

When the baby's acquaintance with the energy taken in through the senses is secured, new jobs can be taken up. The next chapter examines some of them.

4 Temporal Hierarchies: Why Babies do one Thing Rather Than Another

Since there is so much to learn about the world in which we are born, can we find a rationale for a baby choosing to be involved in one activity rather than any other?

Before entering into any activity, a baby needs to know which instruments are required. There are two ways he can use to attain this knowledge. One is through a chance awareness. The other is by attempting to extend the instruments he is already using, either by combining them or by deliberately applying them to an activity that he perceives relates to these instruments. In the life of every baby there is a vast number of each approach.

Why does a baby not set to the challenge of speaking as soon as he is born? Because the activity of speaking must be preceded by the mastery of other activities. For example: it is not necessary to listen to oneself crying, but it is possible, and, if a baby does it, his ear can find in the sounds he hears an involvement that may strike him as worth pursuing. Crying is conscious, and when hearing has become the focus of attention, a bridge can be established between the capacity to make noises and the capacity to recognize them. Because the baby's capacity to make noises is voluntary, he may easily give himself the task of establishing in the ear a new set of criteria concerning sounds.

Once this set of criteria is established, it can serve as a monitor of all utterances — and indeed all speakers use it all the time, forgetting the voluntary part which is now automatic, and depend on the alertness of their hearing and listening to check spontaneously the correctness and adequacy of their spoken words.

Before a baby engages in the task of speaking he has to have solved problems like the above, even though he cannot suspect that it plays any role in the apprenticeship to a language of which he as yet knows nothing.

For another example, consider the kind of steps a baby must master in the process of learning to control the movements of his body. Having been born capable of acting on the muscle tone of all his energized muscles and finding his hands endowed with units that he can activate separately — we call the units fingers — the baby may by chance enter into the dialogue of contracting and relaxing some of his muscles and noting the effect. Once awareness has been brought to the resulting changes, a universe suddenly opens up that takes the baby — through exercises devised by himself — to the knowledge that his hands are instruments for grasping objects, for turning them, for throwing them, for acting upon materials in a number of ways.

For many days this awareness provides the baby with endless opportunities to transform into instruments what he is learning through games. For example, when he notices, while on his back, that he can affect the muscle tone of his lower back and thereby obtain the result of lifting his legs, he becomes an expert at bringing his feet near his face or shoulder — or even at putting his big toe into his mouth. This mastery of what is required in order to act upon the legs permits him to form a right angle between them and his thorax and abdomen.

Now, imagine a baby who can grasp the railings of his crib and hold fast to them, and who can fold his legs up until a right angle is formed: he needs to expend only a small amount of additional energy to find that the rotundity of his buttocks will transform this right angle into another right angle, this time with the body vertical and the legs and thighs lying on the crib. He will have taught himself to sit and to sit up.

This further example of what we shall call a <u>temporal hierarchy</u> — one step building on the last — makes clear that one's consciousness is the key to success in any activity and that without it there is no attempt to entertain such activities nor any chance of success. Parents cannot teach their children any skills that demand a number of prior activities that the parents do not know about. Parents may see that if they do certain things, they help their child <u>to sit</u>, but they don't help him to <u>learn to sit</u>. This he alone can manage, precisely because he alone can know the actual transformations of muscular energy required to reach a particular state.

Much earlier in his life a child has had to learn how to put his thumb in his mouth. This trivial exercise is full of traps and achieved only because consciousness is guided by a body-image, which tells the contracted arm that it is being placed at the proper angle and in the proper place to achieve the entry of the extended thumb in the invisible mouth. Trials and errors are needed to solve this problem, as many facial scratches testify.

Thumb sucking brings us to an interesting example of a baby's choice of an activity. Thumb sucking is not something that a baby is taught from the outside; it is something he teaches himself through his consciousness by developing the appropriate skills over a period of time. But why should a baby want to suck his thumb?

He will not want to before he can do it (even if it occurs in utero as is reported in some cases), but the motivation cannot be solely in this capacity. He could perhaps put his fingers in his nose, or ear, or even his eyes; but he does not do these things. Is it not possible that every baby knows that frictioning his gums reduces the pain caused by the teeth pushing at and breaking through the cartilage of the gums?

The knowledge that relief can be obtained in this way is certainly available to the baby. No one teaches us to press against any part of our body to relieve a neuralgia. The action is such a spontaneous response, known from our intimacy with our soma, that in circumstances such as a rapid descent of a plane, passengers put their fingers in their ears although the action is useless.

That teeth are growing in the gums, and that relief of pain can be obtained by massaging them, could well be the motivation for so many babies in all cultures discovering how to insert their thumb in their mouth. Moreover, if this is done for many months, who can expect that the habit can be easily broken?

Living in Time

Living is the consumption of public time. The inner equivalent of this process can be found in the temporal hierarchies of awarenesses. We need not shift to mysterious notions such as experience and maturity when only awareness is at stake.

Once the awarenesses are present, they can be integrated with subsequent awarenesses. It is not too much to say that every baby knows that he is changing time into experience and that this experience can have a form, an objectification, resulting from the energy mobilized for some new function.

Before a baby knew how to sit, he had many functionings at his disposal that he needed in his attempt to learn to sit. Then, by learning to sit, he added an <u>integrative schema</u> to his awareness, and while all the functionings required are still available to him as before, the act of sitting has brought them into a relationship that gains an existence of its own and can be practiced <u>per se</u>.

So it is when a baby learns to crawl, learns to stand, and learns to walk. None of these achievements is the direct consequence of the existing components. A new schema, as if it were falling upon the baby from the future, makes him consciously reorganize the appropriate competences to display what was not there before.

Integration is the process by which the future affects what already exists. Every baby who finds himself doing one new thing after the other, creating new constellations of existing behaviors for new ends, cannot fail to know himself as living in the future, as meeting the unknown, the unforeseen.

Again, the process is entirely an inner one. Only when a baby knows how to perform certain acts can he find that a similar act is being performed by others — similar, not the same, for the action he sees uses another soma and is perceived from outside, while he knows his own action from inside.

The concept of temporal hierarchies speaks of the necessity for some awareness, some functioning, or some organ to serve as an instrument to generate further awarenesses or even new functionings (corresponding perhaps to some man-made "organ" such as speech). Change or development in the self needs nothing more.

4 Temporal Hierarchies:
Why Babies do one Thing Rather Than Another

The presence of consciousness in a temporal hierarchy usually takes one of three forms. Consciousness can enter into a dialogue with the self as it is now, consciousness can dwell in newly mastered functions, or consciousness can use the totality of the automatic functions. This trinity of the states of consciousness — the yesterday, the today, and the tomorrow of the self — is ours all through our conscious life and is available to everybody. It is the testimony that the individual is a person and can transform himself to take care of what comes.

Because babies know this as the reality of life, they display, as a natural component of their outlook, an attitude that can be called the suspended judgment attitude, which is often lost through faulty education. It is a precious power to have had.

Since the world is full of unknowns, how could a knowing self do anything other than suspend judgment?

What a tremendous power it is to leave to tomorrow the final verdict on what has been lived today!

As babies and young children we know how to do this "naturally," and it allows us to develop the attitudes required by the learning we engage in. Although the process is clearest in the study of the speech of babies, it is not special to that area. Its validity is the result of the temporal nature of life, because we need time to objectify, to become aware of details, to practice. Moreover, so long as this quality of life is known to the self, suspension of judgment will be the attitude taken by the self when engaged in any activity. Proof of such suspension can be found in the absence of a feeling of failure in a child engaged in any true learning. There is no expectation of doing better than one did; there is only the dwelling on what to do next so that inadequate functionings become more adequate to the challenge.

The Tools of Synthesis and Analysis, and of Intuition

It is hard to conceive that the very complex achievements demanded of the very young could result from any blind technique, like trial-and-error. Instead, babies need to develop the tools of understanding that are capable of holding vast masses of data received simultaneously and to interpret rapidly the significance of particular elements. The alternating use of synthesis and analysis is such a tool.

For instance, learning to sit or to crawl, or, earlier still, learning to "spin round one's navel," all involve the synthesis of impulses directed to a large number of muscles, which together end up as a single activity that can be judged for its adequacy and can be selectively altered so as to satisfy a vigilant self. If this were not so, we would be facing continuous miracles.

There are children who crawl before standing or walking, and others who don't. Since this particular learning cannot be inspired by the imitation of all-powerful adults, we can study the simultaneous use of synthesis and analysis in crawling to provide a (temporary) solution to the challenge of locomotion.

To be able to crawl, a baby must know the following, all at the same time: that his skin is in contact with a supporting surface which cancels his weight, <u>and</u> that his contact with this surface can be altered selectively by affecting the tone of specific muscles, <u>and</u> that by pressing on the surface with some parts of himself while lifting some other parts a thrust ahead results, <u>and</u> that this can be repeated, stopped, or altered in a number of ways.

It takes time to learn to crawl, but once learned it can be perfected and taken to truly amazing levels of efficiency for a locomotive skill that will soon be replaced by a very different one.

It is interesting to see babies who have learned to walk still use crawling when they can rely more definitely on this form of locomotion than on walking. If all this were "instinctual," as naive observers say, how could this particular choice of behavior be understood? No learning in human babies can be instinctual. There is always judgment synthesizing the perception of a challenge and the knowledge of the self's capabilities at all levels where awareness has been at work, from conception onwards.

When we think of the complexities of the universe and the short time it takes babies to learn so much, we have to grant to each baby an arsenal of ways of knowing in keeping with the number and diversity of the challenges it confronts.

The caution shown by babies when taking the first steps in any learning is the sign that the knowing self is meeting the unknown, <u>not</u> the sign of a clumsy system suddenly attempting to shift its functionings through accommodation to new stimuli. Babies seize a challenge with all that is available to them and express their grasp by a test to learn if their intuition is correct. As soon as a test is successful, a bolder attempt is made, still in accordance with the intuition. If this is confirmed, consciousness provides analytic, sure knowledge that creates the integrative behavior that makes the challenge part of the system, thereby altering the system.

Intuition is the only way of knowing the unknown through whatever can be grasped of it while still respecting all that cannot be reached analytically at the time. Without intuition no one could do more than respond timidly to discrete stimuli; with it, bolder, encompassing steps are possible.

The Adventures of Babies

We have assumed the success of the first steps, but if there are problems, the suspended-judgment mechanisms make the baby stop in his tracks and consider whether he will postpone further movement in the area of his present concern or attempt alternative solutions. All parents can point to such manifestations of "intelligence" in their child during his pre-verbal stages.

4 Temporal Hierarchies:
Why Babies do one Thing Rather Than Another

For instance, a child's discovery that a rail can be used to take some of the weight of his body if he holds on to it may provide him with the opportunity of preparing for walking — that is, for using certain muscles of the legs and thighs for certain ends. Once a child has enough acquaintance with the balance required to stand without support, he may give himself a new challenge and contract some muscles of only one leg (thus generating an opportunity to fall). If, after the contraction, the baby quickly tries to restore his balance with the same leg, he most likely will end up with his two legs no longer side by side. If he does restore the equilibrium, he will have discovered that balanced standing can be accommodated to a number of different angles of the thigh-leg systems. A repetition of the exercise may result in a new phenomenon, the fact that his body has been successfully displaced from here to there — and the awareness of walking is born.

Some children may take weeks between their first step and the first sequence of steps. This depends on the kind of consciousness that accompanies the discovery of how to restore balance after a failure in the act of walking. If no emotion intervenes, there may be no postponement of the progression from one to more steps, but only the baby knows his state, only he knows what he is focusing upon in all these solitary exercises involving the self as free energy and the self as soma.

Temporal hierarchies are safe instruments for understanding the adventures of babies in their world. These hierarchies allow us to avoid the notions of rigid sequencing or random occurrences, and enable us to look at what actual particular situations demand of learners. It so happens that all of us, or almost all of us, end up doing mostly the same things in almost the same way. But this is only the appearance, and even if we end up at the same place, it does not mean we have followed the same route.

Since each of us lives in time and since the time of one's life belongs to each of us to be spent deliberately for the purpose of being who we can be, with our true endowments in our given environment, we can only follow our own path to obtain a conscious balance and integration of the actual experiencing which was and is ours. Looked at from outside, people are alike; looked at from inside, from the temporal viewpoint, everyone is different. Indeed we are all very different, even if we are twins.

By selecting temporal hierarchies rather than structures as our instrument of description, we have made it possible to have a language that maintains the truth of variety and of singularity without at the same time eliminating a possibility of mutual assimilation. We all have to observe temporal hierarchies to end up being able to do comparable things, but we never end up reproducing the same structure, for the structures are the objectification of sequences in time, and these sequences respect only one demand: that in order to function freely and adequately, what is integrated must exist before it can be integrated.

The Changing World and the Changing Self

We all have to go through our own experiences and no one can live on our behalf. The length of one's life does not change this. Each of us has to learn what has to be part of himself, and in learning, the self is changed. We cannot save time by being instructed, but perhaps we can save time by recognizing and utilizing more effectively the various powers of our self.

There are awarenesses within the self that make us perceive ourselves as changing, or make us perceive in our self the dynamics of change. To live in time is to acknowledge that transformations are the true fabric of our being, that without them we would be annihilated.

Babies as well as adults need to know which transformations make living possible; indeed all persons who survive know them and use them. Babies know that they never see the world except in flux. They do not choose to be lifted and moved around, and the classes of impressions they have of every object and every person are the only truth they know.

It is because of our capacity to stress and to ignore, that recognition is possible in a world in flux. Only in the mind do classes gain a stability. Babies see their parents change clothes, appearance, smell, and so on. They see people come close and disappear, changing appearance in so many ways. This is their true world, which would be chaos if the power of recognition that permits us to ignore elements that can distract and to stress others that generate permanences, was not also available to babies.

"Mother" is a set of impressions that allow her to lead her life in the world — having her bath, dressing up to go out, smelling of soap or perfume or sweat or frying oil, her hair down or up, being so near that only a small bit of her face is visible, or being in the next room, or in her car moving away. Which impression is mother? All and none. No unique image can be evoked and labeled mother.

Instead, sometimes mother is recognized by some smell, sometimes by her voice, sometimes by her smile or by her face. So long as the dominant impression evokes the class, mother will be known, and all the potential associations with her will be available.

These open classes of impressions lend strength to the suspended-judgment attitude, for the baby knows that he does not rule the world around him and that for each class there may be new elements springing from nowhere which will claim a place in it. Mother may have a new dress on, or be very ill for the first time; an unknown visitor with the same name as the baby's may come to his home; father may come back from a journey having grown a beard.

Babies are at peace with change simply because they perceive it as the basis of reality. They know that what they see at a distance will look different when they move towards it or when it moves towards them. Hence, they are not dismayed to see people disappear at the end of a road, and they do not look for an object that disappears unless they relate to it and want to have it again, as may happen with toys lost in their cribs. Young children do not mind accepting the appearance that the moon walks with them as they walk <u>and</u> that it also walks with someone else walking in the opposite direction — which is, indeed, the real set of impressions even if it is not an acceptable result in a logical system free of contradiction.

The moon indeed moves with me when I walk in opposite directions. If I trust my perceptions, I must grant this property to the moon. After all, I did not make the world; I only meet it as it is. When later I make separate categories that I acknowledge to be mutually exclusive and find data that tell me that illusions exist and that I must give more credence to one system than to another, I shall merely separate the two phenomena in my mind.

For me, as for Galileo, "e Pur si muove." The moon does march on, even if it is indifferent to what I do on earth.

*   *   *

In employing the perspective of temporal hierarchies, we give ourselves a chance of seeing wisdom at work on elements other than family, social, and business concerns. Wisdom is displayed by babies at every stage of their dialogues with their successive universes because wisdom is nothing other than the candid recognition of what one is able to do and what one is permitted to do. Wisdom, therefore, is likely to be found in later years if it has been enhanced at all ages by a sense of realism in connection with whatever one is involved in.

It is no harder to be wise in society than it is to use discrimination to cope with teething by putting one's thumb in one's mouth. Each of us is given opportunities to know himself engaged in knowing himself in the world, and hence knowing himself as part of the world. Each opportunity must be taken here and now and not be postponed to later years.

Temporal hierarchies are layers of life, no one better than another, no one more precious than another, but simply one after the other, each giving to a preceding one a position of foundation for others and each giving to a subsequent one a position of integration of others. All must be taken care of consciously and conscientiously in order to bring us health now and later. To this process we have been fitted as human beings.

5 Talking: How Babies Master Sound Making

In our effort to understand babies, we repeatedly have asked one question: "What can babies do on their own without help from others?" Here we are going to consider one activity done by all babies — what indiscriminately is called talking or speaking — and see how much of this activity comes from the baby himself and to see as well what the doing of the activity means to the baby.

At the beginning we must sharply distinguish between talking and speaking. Talking refers to the baby's activities, what he can do entirely on his own. Speaking refers to the activity that the social world helps bring to the self. (Similar distinctions can be made in the areas of sight and hearing. In terms of sight, for example, to look is to mobilize the self in the eye so as to become aware of the bombardment of photons on the retina, an awareness that results in the self seeing. In terms of hearing, to listen is to mobilize the self in the ear so as to be able to hear what reaches the drum.)

In this chapter we focus on talking, and our discussion will first reconsider more systematically a few points made earlier.

When a baby makes sounds in his crib, he will be able to hear them if he wills it (and if his ear and acoustic nerve function properly). As soon as he acknowledges that it is he who is making the sounds, he has at his disposal two sources of information, his throat and his ear, to investigate the world of his own utterances. Because a baby can relate what he hears to what he does, he has the necessary equipment to study his sound-production machinery and make it do what he wants.

From his <u>in utero</u> experience he knows how to affect the muscle tone of every muscle involved in phonation. Hence, he can study separately or in conjunction the parts played by an air flow impinging upon the various components of the chamber that a closed mouth represents. He can slow down the air flow by acting upon his lungs and his chest. He can open his larynx by separating the lips of the vocal cords, or bring them together as close as possible and see what the impact of the air travelling at different speeds does to their vibrating ends.

By displacing his attention to other parts of the chamber, he can know how the dynamics of the air affects them, and learn how variations in the muscle tone of his cheeks, palate, tongue and lips, in various combinations, affect the air flow.

Every baby a few weeks old does this during those hours of crying that no adult any longer understands. And the six- or seven-week old baby is actively taking note of what happens to the flow of air when he voluntarily changes the shape of his outer mouth by acting on the muscle tone of his lips.

Learning at this level is a move towards the mastery of the dynamics involved so that the self is certain it can produce a synthesis of lips, air flow, and so forth. With this knowledge, a baby is equipped to move towards another synthesis, provided only that he can hear.

(Observation of deaf babies a few weeks old may not reveal deafness since the inner awareness of somatic states, our subject so far, is accessible to the baby via his awareness of muscle tone. Indeed, that deaf people can learn to utter what they do not hear guarantees that this way of knowing is open to every child who can "read" energy variations in the organs of phonation through the dynamics of muscle tone.)

Clearly, there is no social component in the language investigation of the baby at the beginning of his life. His knowledge will be factual, in terms of his use of what is available and what can be acted upon within himself. To act on one component of the phonation system produces knowledge of what that component contributes on its own and, by involving it with other parts, knowledge of how its contribution is affected by other contributions.

There are several thousand dialects on earth, a fact that tells us that many, many uses of the same components are possible, some of which have been selected by human groups for the specific purpose of creating languages.

A baby who is not yet involved in social intercourse with the speakers of the language of his environment has no obligation to limit himself to the set of utterances selected for the group. He reaches a level of competence in using his vocal system that is most likely equal to the level of any speaker around, though he may not utter a single sound of the speaker's language when he "speaks" his own unique, un-understandable, and most likely unrecorded language.

Talking is this set of activities, leading to the level of performance so many parents have noticed in their children at around their first birthday.

In the first months of life, when teeth are not yet available, babies utter a number of sounds that are affected only by the tongue, cheeks, palate, and lips. Within the range of choices, some are retained later, but knowledge of the remaining sounds becomes useless because they are not practiced. Since the acquaintance that each of us had with these "foreign" sounds was merely somatic, to try to produce them later may meet with failure (unless one can be assisted to regain the state that regenerates the "lost" knowledge.)

For weeks or months, a baby engaged in his utterances will become knowledgeable about all the variables that are part of these utterances. Their duration, their pitch, their intensity are three of the variables that babies can study, both in terms of the energy required and through the analyzed impacts upon the ear. The two systems of criteria, independent of each other in the beginning, become mutually supportive and interchangeable.

(Deaf people stop at the development of the first system of energy variation, and only later gain intelligence of what can be related to it when they are taught the properties of sound through their eyes and skin.)

For the non-deaf baby, the two systems of conscious experiences are put into correspondence so that the ear and the mouth are functionally connected.

Babies have no difficulty in emitting a sound and noting its impact upon their ear. There is no danger that a baby will confuse this sound with the sounds of the environment since the utterance can take place at any time of the day or night — at times when the baby knows himself to be left alone and can be sure that <u>he</u> and no one else has uttered this sound. He at once gives himself a test by doing it again and, if need be, again and again.

Concentrating on both the production of the sound and its reception, he knows what he does to make the utterance, and almost at once he also perceives the particular alterations in his ear and the part of the brain connected with it. He can therefore keep the two awarenesses connected, or else voluntarily emit a sound and switch his attention to knowing it as an entity reaching his ear. When satisfied that his ear is as good an informant of what his throat does as his own direct contact with the throat (through consciousness), he can relax and let the hearing system keep vigil over the functions of the phonation system. From then on, the ear holds the feedback mechanism to inform consciousness of what the throat is doing when uttering sounds.

Every baby soon knows how to increase or reduce both the volume and the duration of any sound he can produce. Sound now becomes a reality *per se* that consciousness can relate to. When the ear registers one of these sounds, the self acknowledges it for what it is. The baby can also relate and work on repetition and the speed of successive utterances.

Since each of us (people who can read and write included) recognizes the various sounds of our language as sounds regardless of all the other associations they may have for us, these sounds must have objectively distinct properties (which, indeed, can be shown on cathode ray tubes). Sounds must therefore correspond to distinctive objective configurations of the phonation system, the result in turn of distinctive constellations of orders given to the constituent parts of the system. Each baby works on generating these constellations and ensures himself that they are available in the various states in which they can be produced: uttered slowly or quickly, repeated, mingled with other mastered sounds, and so on.

This spectrum of known sounds is a by-product of the work done both at the level of phonation or utterance, and at the level of the ear. But it now is a tool for the baby. The more elements there are in the spectrum, the more can be done with it in terms of sounds *per se*.

For instance, an awareness of the possibility of uttering two different sounds one after the other carries with it the possibility of gaining the awareness that there are two orders for uttering these sounds. When sounded, the perceptible differences in the two orders cannot escape notice. Thus, either deliberately or by chance, a baby can discover that the set of sounds he can utter allows some combinations and permutations. Further, awareness of any change that makes combinations different can lead to the awareness that the change is equivalent to a substitution. Putting these observations together, we cannot say anything other than that babies can become aware of an <u>algebra</u> on the set of their utterances.

This awareness finds its way into other fields as well. When learning to order the various movements of his eyes, or when learning to order the command to his head to turn by definite amounts to catch a sound or a sight, a baby has opportunities to know that the movements are ruled by an algebra in which, for example, movements can be composed to produce other movements, each movement can be canceled by an opposite movement, and each turning can be the outcome of a variety of choices of pairs of turnings.

Readers may feel awkward at the thought that we endow children so young with the capacity to become aware of algebras in their activities. We have no choice, except perhaps to refuse to name as algebra what babies actually do, though their activities are the same activities that mathematicians legitimately refer to as algebras when they are considering abstract sets structured by similar operations.

Babies learning to talk have ample opportunity to relate consciously to the voluntary utterances they make. So how could they escape noticing that they add, subtract, substitute, reverse, combine, repeat, and re-order sounds? How can they escape systematizing their conscious work when the material is all in their hands and intimately known? Is it harder to notice these varieties than to notice what can be done with the ocular muscles or the muscles in the neck?

In generating the thousands of known languages, humanity ultimately resorted to using a small number of sounds for each language — in other words, resorted to using an algebra to produce the many times more numerous words of each language. How could this occur at the beginning of the formation of a language if it was not an endowment of the linguistic mind, that is, if it could not be noticed?

To achieve all these awarenesses we do not need all the sounds of a language: a few can serve equally well. But the fact that no baby is committed to any language leaves him free to play with his powers and increase his arsenal of sounds as well as his arsenal of non-verbal (essentially non-substantive) components.

The key to the entry into a language is in this apprenticeship: the study of the parts of the mouth which correspond to the sounds that are heard. Since one can hear sounds that cannot be uttered (such as thunder, or the noise of a car), babies are aware that what strikes them from the environment can be subdivided into distinctive classes according to whether the sound can actually be reproduced by them.

5 Talking: How Babies Master Sound Making

Languages are sounds related in time to form words and collections of words. Each language — in the stress it gives to each word, in the melody of each sentence, and in intonations — presents elements that can be reached <u>per se</u> without any reference to the labeling component. These extra-verbal elements, having an objective existence, will be reachable as soon as the baby's consciousness is touched by each of them.

But long before speaking the language of the environment, each baby who hears has had the opportunity to note that users of the language utter sounds that are modulated by voices in a manner he has made himself capable of analyzing. He can dedicate himself to knowing as much as he wishes of this material and to learning to reproduce it. While doing this, he discovers that he uses his voice and not a copy of those he has heard, although he can evoke them, and he can recognize them, in actuality or in evocation.

This discovery is one that frees each baby from wanting to do exactly and literally what others do. Even if it was possible, it is not required. Some actors, singular individuals, masters of impersonation, select elements of the voice of some celebrity and produce them sufficiently closely to create an illusion of the other's presence. These actors prove that had all babies chosen to impersonate the people around them, each of us would be speaking to those we address using our voice as they use theirs, and we would end up finally with a group of people having only one voice.

We must therefore grant to each baby that he knows very early that there are verbal and non-verbal elements in all languages and that it is easier to assimilate the latter first.

To learn to <u>talk</u> covers all this.

Since most of us end up ready to learn to <u>speak</u> around a year after birth, it must be during those months that we come to non-verbal conclusions about the best way to approach the language of our environment. The transfer of criteria for phonation from the throat and mouth to the ears is crucial, for we shall be affected through our ears as soon as we lend sense to what people around are saying and have to interpret what we hear in terms of utterance.

This delicate and most effective approach to the subtle material of language is best done at this age simply because consciousness is closest to the soma at the beginning of life. Depending on the extent of our individual dedication, we shall each of us give ourselves for the rest of our lives a greater or a lesser acquaintance with the functionings of the systems involved.

The great singers, the early prodigies of the voice as an instrument, can arise anywhere from any milieu because their origin lies only in having cultivated more than have others, at the stage when intimate acquaintance is possible, those vocal gifts that belong to everybody. In particular, they have mastered the mechanisms that integrate breathing and phonation to those that prolong the emission of sounds, those that affect the distribution of energy along the phrases and modulate them, and those that voluntarily blend the evocation of emotions with other vocal elements. All these attentions, easiest to acquire at an early stage in life, provide the basis for the rapid growth of experience and serve to distinguish these babies from babies who are attracted by other fields of experience and who attend to the awarenesses of sound only enough to enable such babies to learn to speak.

6 Speaking: How Babies Master Language

Most children who learn to talk end up learning to speak one of the codified languages in their environment, however difficult that particular language seems to adults who learn it as a second, or foreign, language. Perhaps there is something in the phase of learning to talk that makes it easy to learn to speak. Certainly to have learned to talk has made it possible for a person to analyze the <u>noises</u> that he hears and to attempt to produce them.

All those who learn to speak must use their own voices to produce those elements, in the packets of energy received by the eardrums, that we call words. It is obvious to every baby acquainted with sounds that words are carried by voices, and can be reached only be ignoring the attributes of voices that do not belong to the words. Hence, no baby will imitate the voices he hears, although he could, but will on the contrary abstract words from their carriers and place them on his voice, which becomes their new vehicle.

Still, no more than an adult can a baby escape the fact that words have no meaning on their own; that they are either totally arbitrary or, in a few instances, formed of combinations of sounds that may have some somatic origin. It has been said, for example, that the Sanskrit word Karma, supposedly summing up one's destiny, starts with a guttural, at the source of phonation, is followed by the conveyor r, produced by the tongue, and ends up with the labial m, which puts the sound in the open as an explosion. But who can say that inchoate tells us anything of its meaning?

That words have no meaning on their own can be ascertained at once by listening to a language one does not know. Hence every learner of a language has to learn that language must first have meanings to refer to.

The bridge between talking and speaking can well be a chance occurrence, as seems to happen to all of us. While practicing his nth sound and amalgamation of sounds, a baby may be uttering a sequence of dadada or mamama or papapa . . . when an adult hears him and exclaims, "Listen, he is calling his father or his mother." And the adult may even believe it. Then all the family surrounds the baby and asks for encores, uttering the sounds the baby is practicing and is therefore acutely aware of.

Thus brought to the baby's awareness is the fact that his ears can recognize what is uttered not only by his mouth but also by the mouths of others. He can now use the combination of the spectrum of sounds he has constructed to analyze what he hears and sees on the mouths of others. He can also now attempt to guide his utterances to evoke the sounds he has heard. His original utterances may be merely truncated replicas of those sounds. Although baby-talk is an incompetent rendition of what is heard, it is as faithful a rendition as the expertise of the talker allows. That so many babies produce the same "distorted" form of words from the environment cannot be due to chance. Just as no one can produce dentals without teeth, no one is able to utter what he does not know how to utter. So babies, doing as usual what they know, utter only what they find in the sounds they hear — those elements that they can recognize through their ear and their throats.

But because the spectrum of sounds expands and listening is acute, babies correct themselves and constantly improve their performance. This improvement is deliberate, the outcome of a reflective self. Some words of the language of the environment are produced correctly at once. This is the case with those words that are repeated syllables, like papa, mama. Other words suggest a way that they might be produced, and babies try, using their breath to produce what their ear catches and their mouths can form. Still other words are not even attempted: they are not yet recognizable to the analytic system formed at that time.

Babies who have perceived so much of the intricate organization of the surrounding world can also perceive that certain gestures often accompany certain utterances. For example, "give it to me," "no," "take this," are often associated with visible indices that can strike the attentive baby. He tests his comprehension by offering his version of the sounds and waits for feedback.

Once he starts on this road, he can easily acquire what he guessed correctly and tested to his own satisfaction, and can "reflect" on how he did it and for what results.

Babies learning to speak know that they don't yet know all the answers, and do not pretend that they do. As usual their attitude of suspended judgment, their keen awareness coupled with selective concentration on elements related to their knowledge, and their focus on perception, makes things happen. Rather than trial-and-error or chance learning, the child's method is that of directed learning which feeds back every piece of progress and makes the child know that he has achieved a definite, certain end.

This occurs even when the end of language is not the aim of the project. Such is the flexibility of the engagement of consciousness in the act of learning that it can be moved without difficulty to another matter that seems interesting. (Who has not taken for intellectual superficiality or immaturity the ease with which young children leave an occupation, including the experience of deep grief, to be utterly taken by what has just met their perception? This power of babies, and sometimes of older children, to identify with a task immediately, is a tool of such importance in learning that we should all acquaint ourselves with it.)

A sequence of words in time presents many intellectual demands. We have to hear each word when it strikes the ear, we have to retain it while we shift to the next word, we have to do this a number of times until the statement is finished, and then hold this statement in the mind to draw out of it its meaning. Once meaning is squeezed out of a statement, the words do not need to be remembered, and the recovery of the energy mobilized for that task begins.

If this is what we all have to do to take in speech, it must also be done by babies.

The way babies find a solution to the challenge of speaking is characteristic of their skills. They begin with one-word statements. "No" is an especially convenient statement, for it conveys meanings while simultaneously protecting the baby-utterer from the aggression of the loving environment and asserting that he is an independent person, a will. Babies also use "no" systematically to discover what is behind the arbitrary sounds floating around. Because speech is in time and because it is only a vehicle for meaning for the user, the learner of speech who has missed something that he feels he needs must resort to some strategy to recreate the lost opportunity. "No" is one of his instruments to have the whole thing dished out again. Normally he will not use it if all is well, if he is content with an intuition and can progress in his work. But how would he otherwise capture that which has vanished into the past? He discovered early enough in his talking that repetition is available to him; now he gets it from others by triggering it with a mere "no."

In the course of a "no"-triggered exchange, baby and adult are engaged in a dialogue that has utterly different meanings for both. While the adult concentrates on the message, the baby concentrates on the vehicle that conveys the message. His is a more complex task, and according to circumstances he may neglect the message in order to be in contact with the vehicle. The environment, so ignorant of the ways of knowing available to a child, so unconcerned with the enormous task he is engaged in, has little interest in helping and often hinders by interpreting the actions of the learner as sheer ill-will. Later, "what?" will play a role similar to "no" and can also become a tool for a nagging child to infuriate his parents.

Quite a number of one-word statements are possible, even if they are not part of the environment's speech habits. If "go," "come," "take," and "eat" are conventional, "give," "hand," "spoon," "alone," are not. Babies choose to utter what they can manage, and by trying out what is convenient to them, they gain an entry into the correspondence of sound and meaning. The environment, delighted by any such feat, responds enthusiastically to sounds that are related to what appearances suggest is an appropriate context for those sounds.

The tolerance of the environment is very helpful to the baby, for once the correspondence between sound and meaning is sufficiently established so that he can release his attention from this task, he can go on with his task of improving utterances.

A baby must do the whole of this work on his own. The environment is so far removed from what he does that all its guesses about his utterances may be wrong, and deliberate help may mean only hindrance. Hence, the best support that parents can give their children in this field is the attitude that anything offered by a baby is miraculous and has to be accepted with grace.

In families with more than one child, parents often turn to their children to decode what the youngest child utters when he is a newcomer to speech. This decoding is possible between children because of the older child's remaining awareness into the process of learning, an awareness that gradually gets buried with age.

At school we are taught grammar as a formal study of the rules of language and many students find it uninteresting or difficult. But no baby could learn his environment's language if he did not make himself sensitive to the many components of grammar — to all of them, in fact. Every baby is properly equipped for such a complicated job because he knows how to suspend judgment, he knows how important it is to give himself to a task, to pay attention, to focus on some point in order to master it, to interpret feedback. He is as sure of the fluctuating nature of the outside world as of his own experience, and he uses his intellectual powers so efficiently that as soon as he knows a little he manages to know a lot.

There is a great deal of creative activity in learning to speak and a great variety in the solutions to the problem of acquiring an existing language. If freedom were not part and parcel of this apprenticeship, the uniqueness of human beings could not be accommodated. Circumstances differ every day for each of us; what people say is unpredictable; so are the demands of situations. Hence, there can be no one-track program to be followed by all children, not even all the children in any one family. Instead, as always, there are temporal hierarchies: the construction of islands of connected awarenesses corresponding to certain criteria and vocabularies, which are then related to chunks of experience in the world; the construction of continents out of these separate islands; the construction of verbal universes with the presence of a unique self using what was given in a unique fashion.

Children, although they end up speaking more or less equally well, start at different ages and follow different routes; they dwell longer in some areas than in others because they find something fascinating in them. Numerals, for instance, may strike one child as having some property resembling the physical learning of climbing steps, and he may master counting, say at the age of two before he gives signs that he has mastered a sentence. When this happens, it gives the impression that the task of counting is easy for some younger children.

The particular task of counting involves a very specific set of demands to be mastered: twelve noises, say, must be retained; they must be put in order; they must then be synchronized with a somatic complex, which could include lifting a leg from one step and putting it on the next and then, with the help of the arm on the banister, lifting the whole body to the new level. However complicated a behavior, it is a limited one and is open to a two year old who engages himself with its components.

Since adults verbalize spontaneously all the time, they provide each child with a large number of opportunities to acknowledge that the sounds he hears uttered by adults are sometimes mysterious and unrelated to anything he can perceive, and at some times concomitant with what he can notice. Nouns are examples of the latter, and he may associate the sound "doggy" with the animal he is familiar with, "glass" with the object used by everybody at meals. But he can also notice that "eat" always recurs when someone is feeding him, and although he cannot use the word because he does not feed people, the possibility is open to him to make sure of its meaning. He simply tests that the word is uttered again if he refuses to open his mouth, and again and again, and used not only by his mother but by anyone confronted with his refusal to open his mouth.

As he continues to work on relating meaning to words that are meaningless <u>per se</u>, and sorts out the words attached to objects and those attached to actions, he can relate to speech in a variety of ways. He has entry into the staccato of phrasing and the temporal melody of language, into the stressing of words and the use of intonation in sentences.

He will find that to speak (that is, to produce the complex of sounds produced by the people of his environment) he needs to synthesize the components that he can reach separately. Only such a synthesis enables him to know, for example, that the imperative form of a verb requires that he be directed in a total way to the awareness associated with a command about, say, opening his mouth (eat!), moving his whole body (come!), bending his head when being shampooed (bend!), turning his head to let mother see whether the ears are clean (turn!). The concomitants of the voice force awareness both of a verbal form (here the imperative) and of the particular sound as it relates to the particular action he is involved in.

The perception of an object as belonging to a class — that, say, a collie is a dog just as a dachshund is — is possible because of the fact that we know <u>only</u> classes of impressions that are perceived to belong to each other. We produce the concept of an object with only enough precision to accommodate all the related impressions. The same "looseness" is associated spontaneously with words and remains a property of vocabulary. It is a necessary association. Words can be submitted to some vocal transformations without affecting meaning (for example, can be spoken by louder or softer voices), and to other vocal transformations that do affect the meaning (for example, when used to warn, to threaten, to promise). All this educates every baby to watch for all the components that maintain or affect meaning, adding further to the complexity of the task, but also adding power to the tool that is forged.

To comprehend nouns the learning child must associate classes to them simply because he knows that the world is not ruled by him and that he cannot call a thing by any word he chooses. His mistake of addressing any male visitor as "dad" reveals his state of mind and shows the conflict between his learning of nouns and of some social factor that he has not yet perceived. Although all dogs are called "dog" — and using "dog" for a cat (easily taken to belong to the same class) is normal in this context — the use of "dad" for every person is forbidden, for the word refers to an invisible characteristic, a relationship that, indeed, will be met again and again, thus generating a class but a class of pairs of individuals. The baby must refrain from using "dad" for every man, but will accept later that each person can use "dad" when referring to different people (in a few exceptional situations, to the same person). The shock of the awareness that nouns are for classes of individual objects and also for classes of pairs keeps each baby alert, which in turn helps make the learning of the language possible.

Awareness of transformation is necessary in order to penetrate the mysteries buried in languages. Pronouns are substitutes for nouns; yet there are very few pronouns compared with the many nouns, and they are "passe-partout" words. "I" can be used by everyone, but it means someone else when heard and means oneself when uttered. Pronouns are used continually by people in the environment and because they are small words that can be isolated from the rest, they usually get attention quite early. "I" is an exception, and offers difficulties of another kind. For the subject to name himself as if he were an object provides a considerable challenge that is normally solved only when children have been speaking for some time.

Once the speakers of a language have noted that speech is an effective tool of expression, they will use it in one way when they refer to past experience and in another way to refer to the future. Every baby who, like any adult, knows when the thing talked about is being evoked rather than perceived, will know what makes him notice the words that refer to the past, or the future, and he will establish a sensitivity to tenses in the flow of words. The referentials, being repeatedly used, become second nature, and criteria at the level of speech replace criteria of awareness. A particular sound enclosed among the sounds that form a sentence triggers the inner climate that is compatible with the meanings associated with the sentence Thus we reject, "I'll see you yesterday," but accept "I'll see you later," even though the sentences have the same valid form.

For a young child, as for the adult, it is the inner transformations of the self that make a sentence "correct" — and that enables it to be passed by the internal censors that have changed criteria into automatic feedback mechanisms.

Children in their first three years or so show that they are busy in understanding consciously how the tenses are formed, and very many English-speaking children deliberately interfere with the language. They regularize past tenses and say "breaked" for "broke" or "broken," "taked" for "taken," "teared" for "torn," although they do not hear these words said. Such initiative must force students of early childhood to stop thinking that the act of learning one's native language is the result of simply saying what the people in the environment say.

In fact, without a clear concept of "relativity" young children would not learn the use of, say, possessive adjectives and pronouns. If a mother says to a baby, "This is your nose," why should he not say the same words when pointing at his nose? Instead, he changes the expression and says, "This is my nose." If he hears, "You are on my right," what he must finally say is, "I am on your left," a sentence that contains only the word on in common with the previous one.

Through their intellectual powers children invent more than the regular forms for the past tense of irregular verbs. They may be struck by other forms they hear and try to use them to express what they feel. All parents have scores of examples to illustrate the verbal initiative of young children. The following example is crystal clear: A boy, having heard his mother say to him, "Come with me," and having heard himself say, "Me talking," knows that me can be used by other people and by himself. On other occasions he may note that "both" is used to refer to two people (or two things) simultaneously. Thus, he may take his mother's hand and say, "<u>Both of me</u> go down to get the mail." Logically, "both of me" is as correct as "both of us," but only the latter has been adopted.

The real criterion for knowing a language is the capacity to transform statements that are heard into the proper, and perhaps very different, statements that must be uttered by a speaker to convey the same meaning.

At a certain age, children who are still learning the basics of their native language want to give themselves the criterion by which to judge whether they can produce as good a flow of words as their older siblings or their parents.

Some children play the game of "echoing" — repeating with the same speed and intonations everything that people around them say. For weeks on end children test their ability to utter anything and everything they hear immediately after it is uttered by someone else. This very annoying echo creates tension in homes where it is not understood as being a reasonable way of making sure that certain components of speech (flow and intonations) are mastered. But as abruptly as it is taken up, it is dropped, and echoing reappears only much later as a game, or in order to annoy someone deliberately.

It is relatively easy for children in their early childhood to speak a number of languages to a certain level of efficiency. It is possible to conceive of an environment where adults deliberately replace the value of supremacy for one language with the value that their children should know as many languages as possible to the same level of competence.

This is not expecting too much because the greatest job in learning to speak is done for one language and can be simply transferred to other languages. Vocabulary acquisition is the least of the demands in the learning of a new language. Hence, if we learn languages at a time when we are intimately engaged in the study of one, we find access to all the others just as easily. If we start to meet language early, there is no loss of the necessary powers when we go from one language to the next, and to the next. Nor do these powers disappear. We can maintain the capacity for learning more languages to any age.

To sum up the substance of this chapter, we can say that we have seen that only consciousness can sort out the manifold demands in the task of learning to speak and develop the proper, adequate tools in terms of sensitivity, functioning, observation, daring, testing, and acceptance of adequacy.

The example of learning to speak is a valuable illustration of the powers of children; it also shows us that the conscious self alone can do this enormous job while other tasks are being worked on at the same time. The conscious self is the same one that did the various jobs in the soma, and the one that will do the many jobs to come. After learning to speak the conscious self not only finds itself owning a language that can be used but, more importantly, finds itself with the techniques of learning that were developed to meet and integrate the unknown.

Babies learn to speak because they do all the right things in agreement with the rest of their investigations of the surrounding world. They perceive truth and know that words are labels not to be confused with the things associated with them.

7 Learning Other Things: Children Investigating Their Universe

There are many examples of learning in early childhood, but adults are mostly unaware of their existence and their meaning for growth.

For example, most of what looks like idle play is the methodical examination of an unformulated question. The question becomes clearer if one asks: "What does the child need to know that he can get from this activity?"

In many kitchens where pots and pans are within reach of babies, it is possible to see a baby concentrate on playing with this equipment for days if mother allows him and no other brother or sister spoils the game. What is there to find out in a set of pots and pans?

If the pots have lids, can one learn, simply by looking, which lid belongs to which pan? And if only one lid belongs to a particular pan, what do the other lids have that can be isolated? Is it possible to classify the lids in a series?

Can one pan be put inside another? When this is possible, is it possible to reverse the order? Can one use all the pans in one series?

Can one arrive at an arrangement that includes all the pans and also the largest number of lids?

Is there only one solution?

Can one learn such things in a manner that extends the power of the mind — that is, allows one to see that, whatever the answers, there were also awarenesses that were valid and not only for pans?

At any stage in this study, the baby could be diverted and make concomitant discoveries. The noise (that terrible noise for the environment) can become the object of the baby's attention. Do lids vibrate when struck? What stops the vibration? How long is the vibration perceptible if left to continue? Is the noise made by a lid that is too small to cover a particular pan different from the noise made by a larger lid when the two fall on, or touch, a given pan? How does one release a lid or a pan to produce the loudest sound in the various combinations of pans and lids? Is this sound affected by the distance the lid travels? Does the height from which a lid is dropped affect the noise it makes? Does the

7 Learning Other Things: Children Investigating Their Universe

energy with which it is handled affect the level of noise? Can one strike a number of pans and produce recognizable sounds? Is the kitchen filled only with noise or can a kind of harmony be produced?

What about the weight of the pots and pans? Can one's hand lift any of them? Where does one place one's fingers? Is the thumb treated in a special way? Is one hand sufficient? If not, where must the second hand be placed to make lifting the smoothest, the fastest, the least tiring?

Of course, not all children go through the same experiences or ask the same non-verbal questions, but all get involved in games with household appliances that permit them to ask similar questions and to work towards complete answers.

Every child, being a learning system, goes straight to every situation in order to explore what can be known about it. To know finished products, it is necessary to analyze them by breaking them up. If children normally break things rather than consider that they should put them back together, it is simply because the integrative schema of these things is inaccessible to them. On the other hand, in all households (as well as in Headstart or Child Care Centers) observers can notice how quickly most children master commercial jigsaw puzzles and can even put them together while conversing with each other, as if the puzzles were no longer a challenge. Perhaps they never were, for an organizing clue is present and can easily be picked up.

For children of that age, the boundary separating the natural and social environments is blurred. A loud shout from an angry mother, or a threat from a teased sibling, or the noise of a police car siren, are both part of the natural and the human environment. A kick is as real as a table, and some words more hurtful than objects.

Hence, we can expect children to enter very early on into dialogues with all sorts of people in all sorts of ways, just because they want to know, and need to know in order to direct their lives in the world and meet the unpredictable and the unknown.

Teasing is used universally by children as a tool to estimate the boundaries of other people's love for a child's freedom to function; it tests what the children themselves are prepared to fight for. Even in the last category, there are distinctions to discover: <u>how hard am I prepared to fight for this or that?</u>

How to use crying as a deliberate weapon to enlist support from parents against someone else is another dialogue, and from this a child explores justice, fairness, bias, favoritism, and so on.

Of particular interest in the area of child-adult relations is the readiness of young people to accept that adults should dictate what they, the children, do. In homes where no spanking exists, or any other abuse by parents of their physical power or their economic and social know-hows, it is still clear to children that some things must be done, and the children obey as easily as do those who are threatened. This perception of one's interest as a

7 Learning Other Things: Children Investigating Their Universe

member of a group, and the acceptance of the fact that to stop a game to eat or go out is part of the order of things, is a gift children make in the cause of family peace. To understand it as the outcome of the working of fear and a sense within the child of his own inferiority, is not to do justice to facts. Since children learn to say "no" so early to protect themselves from pressure and to warn adults that they can create trouble, the basis of this spontaneous obedience can only be the children's perception of some attributes which the environment has granted to them and which is compatible with their freedom of learning. Children know that they are left alone to do lots of things and to grow in awareness. They know they are able to do today what they were unable to do not so long ago, and they comment on it, verbally or otherwise, very early. Their vision of the environment is balanced, one of give and take, and they know they receive a lot. They see people stop what they are doing to attend to their needs; they can be clumsy and make messes and are not necessarily scolded. Such responsiveness is part of their living and has features they can note; the recognition does not require being schooled, only awareness.

Hence, as children develop a _natural_ place for themselves, reconciling balance, gravitational pulls, chains of movements, taking account of who is to occupy what portion of space, they also develop a _social_ place, unless distortions crop up and generate problems that could otherwise have been avoided by common sense.

Children take an astonishingly long time to learn to control their sphincters. Some need years — up to 14 in some cases — even though the task seems so easy compared with the problem of learning to speak, which is normally done so rapidly. Learning sphincter control is a mixture of biological and social components, and there lies the confusion, for children and observers alike. The biological part requires only awareness. Sphincters are voluntary muscles, and they are kept closed while the bladder and the rectum fill up.

The additional, social part, is to hold them closed when otherwise they would automatically open. For months no one asked the baby to restrain himself. He was either free, like animals on a farm, to relieve himself at any moment or was given diapers to make the cleaning of the mess easier for adults. He was not required — the social demand — to learn to interfere at the moment of evacuation through the accessible muscle tone of his sphincters.

It is possible that a child, because of his awareness of himself, may arrive on his own at the conclusion that such interference here and now, and only for a few moments, can save him inconveniences he himself notices — for example, that diapers are a nuisance, or that the smell of a mess or the wetness of a surface on which he wants to go on playing are unpleasant. So he may enter into a dialogue through his will with these sphincters and place them under control. But usually the decision to do so is generated by outside sources, and what a few do on their own, bed wetters do much later when sensitive to social shame (or, it could be, when capable of understanding the working of their will, which at last provides the motivation). Much later does not mean differently! The job is the same: a certain muscle tone must be maintained at a level required by the function.

7 Learning Other Things: Children Investigating Their Universe

When small children learn to climb chairs, sofas, and beds, they concentrate fully on mobilizing all they have to meet the new challenge. Intelligence as well as perception is required to find the places to hold on to, the arrangement of limbs, the muscles to affect and in what way. Children who manage to find themselves on a chair or a bed do not quite believe it (their smile of triumph is not one of complacency), and they climb down at once using gravity, thereby learning that descending is an entirely different exercise than the one they are studying — and try again to climb up. Once, twice, or a few times more, and they are <u>certain</u> they have mastered this challenge. They turn to another one, which may require the new integrated skill.

What a subtle and in-depth acquaintance with one's soma is implied by the act of lifting oneself from the ground — by the act that is lumped together with other acts under the name of jumping! The first time a child feels confident that he can enter the field of jumping must be when he has deliberately synthesized the awarenesses that result from standing and walking with those that result from being lifted, from flexing muscles, and so forth. Intimate knowledge of his weight, and of how to increase the energy of the appropriate muscles <u>in toto</u> so as to overcome his weight, give the signal to start attempting the synthesis, first virtually at the level of awareness of energy, then actually.

The virtual action necessarily precedes the actual action, for there is no trial-and-error period, and none is needed. Awarenesses are available and are reachable in any detail, and a child can say to himself, "I can jump," even before he has lifted himself from the floor. He has solved the problem with his somatic intelligence, that is, through the knowledge and understanding of what is involved. This work makes certain that the right amount of energy will be displaced to the proper muscles, in conjunction with the potential energy available in the solid floor or ground, in lifting one's body from the launching pad.

Each child can try again and again, as many times as the energy available in the soma permits. Some children will acknowledge that they have mastered the new skill at once; others may not believe themselves, so marvelous is the feeling of jumping, and they give themselves further chances to make sure of its presence in their battery of skills.

Learning something new never repeats what was previously learned simply because the self who engages in the next exercise has a different awareness of himself than he did before he acquired the preceding skill. It is always a different, more experienced child who attempts the next exercise; hence, he makes the new challenge he gives himself into a new problem. He is bolder, and he cannot be content with the same pace of progress. He does not accept a lesser task than the one he already has solved.

If he can walk forward, he wants to walk backwards. If he can walk, why not place his feet on certain marks? The sidewalks suddenly become inspiring because of all the lines on them. If he can jump with two feet, can he hop on one? Can he hop backwards, or is it too hazardous? Can he take more than one

7 Learning Other Things: Children Investigating Their Universe

step at a time climbing stairs? Or go down backwards? When will the banister become a means of going downstairs?

All these adventures, and many more, strike his imagination and solicit him to enter them.

A tacit pattern of learning emerges for each of them: cautious, marginal entry so as to explore where the stepping-stones for the activity can be found; then wholehearted investigation of the field, accepting errors as guides and putting things right immediately because the proper feedback mechanisms have been deliberately placed to monitor each activity; then further testing of the mastery of all parts of the activity before one declares oneself satisfied with what one has done. Mastery is always the aim, and this is required before the skill can function — when the skill is integrated with all that was there before and the new person enters a wider challenge to test himself.

This four-part sequence of learning — contact, analysis, mastery, application — which ends up with an awareness of oneself owning a new power, is manifested by everybody as they acquire any skill which will become automatic after the mastery of it is acquired. (Automatic, as we know, means that the brain has been educated to respond to the special apprehension of the stimuli and that the minimum of awareness needed to monitor the new functioning for the self is left in the psychosomatic system just constructed.)

Contact with life is the generator of learning, which in turn generates more conscious life and more conscious living. Any child alone never stops being challenged by some aspect of life and displays <u>curiosity</u> — synonymous with readiness to enter a new field; <u>interest</u> — synonymous with being engaged in the activity; <u>enthusiasm</u> — synonymous with the mobilization of energy for the job on hand.

Through learning, a child becomes <u>more himself</u> (although he has used up energy in the process). He knows this himself, and he gladly entertains the possibility of learning by involving himself in scores of games that seem to be ends in themselves but are in actuality the expression of the child's state of involvement with the new activity. Games are the creation of the players, and in early childhood they are concerned with what children end up owning in the various fields of the self's expression.

The motivation is clear to the player, and he is attracted as long as the challenge asks him to extend himself. As soon as the challenge is seen as too easy, the game is dropped.

It is possible that one and the same game is varied enough to match the evolution of the child's successive masteries. For instance, if he has a ball and throws it, and notices that the direction in which it goes and the distance at which it falls depend on what he does, then games of throwing become of interest to him, and he happily engages in them — at first simply to give him practice with holding the ball; then in finding how the actions of his thumb, his wrist, and his forearm muscles affect its direction; and later how his arm provides the energy to cover the distance.

Other games with a ball will coordinate his arms and hands so that he can catch a ball thrown at him, and for years he will practice to improve himself as a catcher.

When babies who have learned to walk want pretexts for running, they throw a ball ahead or kick it, and then run after it. Not a very amusing game indeed; it seems it cannot be fun at all. But it is greatly enjoyed by the solitary player: to give himself a reason for running, he pursues a ball he has kicked!

These games that emerge spontaneously are soon added to by games that involve more than one person. Observation of young children's games will show that each partner plays his game not as a part in a collective endeavor but as if it were created and played for him alone; the others are instruments for his end. Since each is happy exploiting the others, the game can go on. But beware! If anyone does not conform to the expected pattern, he is ousted without hesitation. Game partnerships can end as abruptly as they started. Children at play are not friends, only pawns to serve the cause of each other. Shared group interest is only the appearance, not the reality. The anger of small children playing a family game when their luck is not favorable will prove this to anyone. Small children play only on their terms, mainly because their interest is neither social nor economic but concerns only what they can learn (which may be hidden from their older partners).

Brothers and sisters whose ages differ by more than about three years rarely have common interests. They play "together" only on the older's terms, and the benefit for the younger is mainly in the inspiration he obtains from his admiration of the elder's skill. Since no enjoyment is possible from a game with another who is much more skilled than oneself — and children certainly attempt to be involved in their elders' games — we must accept that in such situations the pattern of the future descending into the present is clearly making its demands on young people. What they are unable to do now but is nevertheless not too alien, can find its roots in a part of their functionings and provide an opening for the descent of that which needs to be realized.

It is in this sense that we hold that, through learning, one becomes <u>more oneself</u>. The potential is actualized.

But not <u>any</u> potential, only that which is ripe for realization.

Now, many, many details of what children do to take the place in the world that is uniquely theirs have not been considered. A number of the details are already part of the arsenal of observers who have looked into this vast continent, still little chartered. Here and there some keen lover of the features of childhood has made a landing and harvested an astonishing crop. Maria Montessori and Jean Emile Marcault are among them. The first is well know as a name, but not read; the second, although one of the most profound thinkers of this century, is known to very few. They, and perhaps a few other observers, have told us that the world of childhood has to be entered on tiptoe and not with the heavy tread of laboratory technicians seeking only the confirmation of their visions; has to be entered with every tentacle and sensor alerted and not with a ready-made theory that filters out what cannot be reconciled to it; has to be entered with love and respect for the person, who is as complete at every stage of childhood as he will be at any adult age and stage.

8 The Love that Babies and Young Children Need

If parents love babies without being asked, where are the signs that inform the parents that their love is what children need?

There are two terms in the relationship. Parents do what they want, and this is said to be what their children need. But in fact babies do not know what their parents think, do not know what to expect and what there is to expect. Hence, they do not indulge in any expectation, and they act in relation to parents as they do in relation to all their other involvements.

Not being equipped to procure food for themselves, their survival depends on being fed. They accept food and do not have to be grateful for it; so long as it is given to them, why should they think that the gift is conditional upon any form of return? Indeed, there is no such awareness in them, and adults invented the notion of "maternal instinct" to place squarely on mothers the totality of the responsibility for keeping babies alive. (Cuckoos are frowned upon because they leave their eggs in the nests of other birds. Similarly, everybody considers mothers who abandon their children to be acting unnaturally.) To find out what babies actually need in terms of love we must look beyond their survival needs, which include feeding, cleaning, and protection against the elements. They are clearly not the children's responsibility — the very young are fearless in their innocence and, because they want to know something, can put a cockroach in their mouth or be fascinated by an avalanche coming their way — and can be dealt with by people who already know how to satisfy them.

The examination of what children need is delicate because we are engaged in looking at what is not visible. If this examination can be carried out, readers will see two things at once: one, why children face dangers that no one appreciates; two, why this has remained unknown for so long.

What are the facts with which we must deal?

Each of us is engaged in his own life and knows his own concerns much more directly than he knows what other people are engaged in. The superimposition of all these individual frames of references creates the state of affairs we are in. Most of us, including babies, mainly comprehend what we have equipped ourselves for and what we connect with. In these areas we are more able to be alert and to respond to the impacts that reach us than in the areas for which we have little or very often no preparation.

8 The Love that Babies and Young Children Need

Time structures the universe into three layers for each of us. We can cope with what involves our past, and perhaps also with our present, but we can cope with what is connected to our future only by good luck. This state of affairs directs our examination of the love needed by babies — or anyone.

Adults express their love for their children by letting the children judge for themselves what they need to be engaged in, according to the way the challenge strikes them, at the pace that is theirs, and until they are satisfied that they have done the job to the best of their ability, insight, and opportunities. *This is love in relation to the children's past and present.*

To say that, for this stage, "children know best," is no indulgence. It is simply a statement of recognition that only the child's own self is in his bag and that the outsider can only surmise the particular connection that exists between the self and its manifestations.

We already leave children alone, as a matter of course, in all areas where we have absolutely no idea what goes on — for example, during the first weeks after birth (unless we notice a disease and then attempt a remedy in our terms). And on the whole, each of us (as a child) manages quite well.

Can we do the same in areas where we have partial access? For example, when babies start to walk or run, can we love them enough to trust them rather than be anxious that they may fall and hurt themselves? Anxious love is one form of love babies do not need. A vigilant parent can be ready to assist in case of any unforeseen trouble but keeps from interfering otherwise. *Love then expresses itself in the restraint exercised by the parent upon himself.*

Children, like adults, cannot verbalize all that goes on in them all day long. Hence, people in the environment can be informed of what goes on in a baby only if they watch, attempt to get correct insights into what children do with themselves, and then test any hypothesis in order to be true to the requirements of the moment. *Love is expressed in these cases as respect for the child's activity.*

If it is true that adults know better in certain cases, it is still respect for truth that makes one's love intervene so as to avoid a particular danger, and intervention of this kind leaves no trauma.

Trauma is caused by the conflict of wills: parents and children wanting to assert themselves rather than, for the parent, serving the cause of growth of the child and, for the child, seeking true knowledge of his parent. Trauma is avoided by love, but *love needs to be enlightened by truth.* In this principle, parents have a criterion to help them know whether an act of their intervention is an act of love or the result of some other movement of the self.

It is true that children, for years, are smaller than their parents and that parents have powers children do not as yet have and cannot, for some time, even conceive that they some day might have. This single discrepancy generates in children an inner climate of admiration that can serve their growth if adults manage to learn how to enter it and let it guide them in the parent-child relationship. The admiration is not contrived; its genuineness generates inspiration and the belief that grown-ups can do what only super-beings can do. Children naturally make their parents into heroes and omnipotent beings. This gift will last as long as the distance in power between them is a fact that is verifiable every day. The attitude rarely survives in teenagers, and head-on fights between the generations may result. But even very young children can discover the lack of truth, the pretense of morally weak parents, and can suffer the shock of disillusionment, often leading to mental uncertainty and confusion.

Children do not need to concentrate on family problems. They have something else to do, more important for their true preparation for living in the complex and demanding world they were born into. But if they cannot escape being present and witnessing what is utterly incomprehensible to them, their perception of it and their consciousness are struck differently and they respond in ways that may be unpredictable but fall within understandable forms. Their need for peace, so as to be able to go on with what matters to them, and their wish that the disturbing elements would vanish join to distort the functioning of their sense of truth and make them accept what they are not equipped to reject: that the world is bad, or grown-ups irrational, or God unreliable, or reality a dream, and so on.

To give up reliance on one's sense of truth is the greatest traumatism for anyone, for its guidance is needed at every moment and at all ages. The parent who knows how to respect truth and how to respect the functioning of the sense of truth in his children is giving them the love they need most, the only form that cannot be replaced by anything else. Sentimentality is, in a way, the opposite of this kind of respect. Wavering for one's own convenience also denies the consideration of truth. Truth can be taken into account rightly and more easily than any other demand in one's life. This is because we all have a sense of truth and use it from the beginning of life, knowing its functioning intimately.

Parents often mistakenly regard a thorough involvement of their children in activities cogent to their own level of consciousness as a lack of perception of the rest of the universe. Hence, they do not take the necessary precautions to avoid situations in which their children may have to perceive what they may not comprehend, and parents use the excuse that children lack awareness when they do not behave conveniently.

The love children need most is connected with knowing the dynamics of what is immanent yet transcendental to them. To grow up normally is to bring part of the immanently transcendental to the level of the consciously mastered.

This does not mean that children do not also need the love that corresponds to the truth of feelings, but the absence of this love is less damaging to them because the sturdy self of a functioning baby in contact with his sense of truth can cope with realities at his level. A loved baby will not miss a dead or absent father; he will not suffer much if he is fed the foodstuffs of his community even if some vitamins or calories are missing; he will not mind social conditions that may later appear appalling to him: in short, he will find the environment acceptable, whatever it is. But he cannot make sense of the sometimes gentle father who becomes unpredictably violent for reasons beyond him; or of the sometimes smiling, sometimes screaming mother whose mood is governed by causes invisible to him; and so on. The universe is indeed sliced "horizontally" for him into two levels, and he is at peace in one, whatever happens, because he lives in it — it is his world; but he is totally vulnerable in the other because he does not dwell in it, although he is capable of perceiving appearances in it.

For the first level, love is best expressed by considering a child as a complete person, having as much access to criteria as any other person, however old. For the second, love requires forms that distinguish adults from children and places different responsibilities on them.

Rather than ask children to obey them blindly or, at the other extreme, exercise no authority at all, parents who know that children have important jobs to do and that they cannot do them all at once will structure their relationship to their children, adopting a hands-off attitude in some sectors and a very careful and subtle involvement in others.

Children need at all stages a love that leads to responsibility coupled with autonomy and independence, love that frees and is therefore joyful. To provide this love, parents need to be genuinely themselves and sensitively need to avoid generating experiences that throw children into the layers of consciousness where they have had no practice. Parents who are not genuinely themselves are actors all the time, and such a sustained artificiality cannot but translate itself in a hollowness that frightens the innocent child engaged in seriously living his life. If parents are not sensitive to what they generate, how can they avoid offering their offspring situations where appearances replace truth?

There are many dangers when this happens:

1. Appearances are sometimes the truth, sometimes not, and no one can trust appearances fully, particularly when there is no access to the criteria of truth in that field.

2. Without a basis for judgment, what is one to do? Accept randomness? Guess and count on luck to be right? Lose all foundation for one's confidence in operating correctly in that field?

3. To need to refer continually to others for acceptance of one's conclusions eliminates the possibility of maintaining an integrated self.

In a universe in flux, where appearances cannot be trusted and the only basis for mental — and hence total — health is to be an integrated self, it is imperative to maintain the functioning of one's sense of truth all through life.

It is the role of love that moves parents to throw bridges of truth between the future and the present in their children's lives and to acknowledge that until around adolescence, they, the parents, must protect their children from being pressed by the immanent that is not yet within their children's reach. This love permits the smooth descent of the future into the present and permits the task of meeting the unknown to be a gradual integration of what one is with what one will be. This is what has taken place since the egg was formed, and therefore it reveals accurately that children are expert at doing by themselves and what they do spontaneously.

Love for a child at the beginning of his life makes parents eliminate the obstacles to his survival on the somatic level; almost all parents know how to do this, even if they need a hint here and there. Then, as sheer survival is pushed one or two stages beneath the visible surface, parents learn to relate differently to their child, who now has other needs, and they learn to provide the psychic and spiritual environment that will make him able to cope better with the world at large. Love makes adults give up using some of their time for themselves and for their own ends and give it instead to play with their children.

Now games may be created only to assist their children's growth with no challenge to the parents, but the games can have some attraction for the curious parent. A shift of view towards allowing all games a chance to school <u>parents</u> in the study of their children's functioning may make all the difference to parents' lives and to the way they knowingly serve their children. Love is needed to make that shift. It can operate by reviving in parents a childhood attitude: the need to know — but this time to know their children as they are, here and now, and to eliminate any relationship with them based on an <u>a priori</u> model.

Parents' love makes them sensitive to the interference in the vital activities of their children caused by the social elements in the family. Clearly, the running of a house makes demands on parents, who in turn are entitled to their own life. Yet, that the right of parents to their own life often becomes an encroachment on the life of their children can be seen in the supremacy usually granted to dinner over all the other activities of everyone at home. Everything must stop for dinner, and everyone must rush to the table. Only love can make one see that this ritual could be the source of a distortion of reality in which one thing always subordinates all others. Further, only love can make one see that a discussion of this situation leading to a rationalization justifying the imposition of a timetable is only a rationalization and may not really serve the best interest of the family members. Love is needed because the total picture is difficult to see.

To say that it takes love to prepare a dinner, that love is a give-and-take, and that children must learn to give not only take, is precisely the problem for which love is needed. Only love can make one see that there may be other ways of bringing give-and-take to a child's notice than forcing the acceptance of a dinner timetable, that to call children to dinner demands the abandonment of what they may be engrossed in and so can generate a slow relinquishment of the respect for what other people are doing. The shift is not based on true criteria but is a habit that may or may not make sense to particular children.

Love is required to be more conscious when confrontations arise. In confrontations, parents and children find their school for love. Here also are the opportunities to find out how to learn to take other people into account. Preaching and talking blur the issues. To take other people into account — as, say, policemen do — is not love. The terms must be reversed. To love <u>makes</u> one take people into account and is the method mankind has developed to transcend self-interest and give reality to the interests of others. Love makes one creative in situations that conflict with the profound knowledge that all that happens to oneself is noticeable and co-extensive with reality for oneself but may not be for others. Love fertilizes one's imagination and places in oneself the presence of others as autonomous beings who are endowed with much one knows to be attributes of oneself — in particular, feelings, a will, and a vision of the world. Through this love, by making oneself move to accept others, others accept oneself. The respect for their reality and all that they are engaged in is a form that love can take and a channel for its expression.

But because to love truly is demanding and to have children is not, there is no relation between being a parent and loving one's children, except only in the sense that animals can be said to love and protect their offspring. Even there, perhaps the only true act of love is to free the cub when he can survive by himself.

For man, love is a universe to enter and dwell in, kept intact only by the acts of will that are needed to sustain it. Parents' love is no more regulated than lovers' love. It only truly exists when it is capable of continuously renewing the vigilance that makes the other's reality never quit one's consciousness. When love is in that state, it does not lose contact with this reality and does not need to be argued about. It recognizes itself while it molds itself to the ever-changing awareness of the living being one is relating to.

Children need this love and can do without all the others. To produce a humanity, a society as vast as the earth in which all beings are equal because each is consciousness at work, this love is required. The acceptance of this love by more and more people is a measure of the movement towards humanity. Since parents and children are the people who compose the population of our world, their awakening to the fact that the love they need and the love they aspire to are one and the same, may generate in them the willingness to change so as <u>to be</u> that love — in the same sense as one <u>is</u> one's soma.

A humanity cannot exist beside or outside persons. The education of love, for love, is education of an awareness with two poles: oneself the lover and the others to be loved. When everyone loves, no one has to point the way. Things take care of themselves.

Part II

Of Boys and Girls

Introduction

Once a young child has explored, and made his or her own, the multitude of experiences which fill early childhood and make each five-year-old an extremely competent user of somatic functionings (as diverse as the functionings involved in talking, walking, seeing, hearing), there next stands the universe beyond these first reachings, the universe of second childhood. All parents are struck by the physical functional changes which are visible in their children between the ages of, say, five and seven. They are struck, in particular, by the new daring shown in some actions, daring which can only exist if there is an increased mastery by the self over its soma and its functionings.

The age we are concerned with in this section can be called "the age of stressing action as a way of knowing" — of knowing both oneself and the dynamic universe in which one finds oneself. During these years, boys and girls give their universe new dimensions, construct it with their own substance, and make it resemble their image.

Part II
Of Boys and Girls

But is there so much to find out about during this period that five or six years are required from each of us to learn it, even though we are most efficient learning systems? This is what the following chapters will show.

9 Perception at the Service of Action: Marbles and Hopscotch

A very young child, who has so much to acquire in the field of skill in order to enter a world inhabited by people of all ages who are engaged in many activities at many different levels of performance, has to find within himself the means to make sense of what he sees in the environment. He has to learn to surrender to what he perceives, to be ready to make mistakes and to try again because he knows he does not yet know exactly what to do with himself.

This yielding to the truth of a situation, this attitude of suspended judgment, this good will which leads a baby to try even when the result is unknown or unsure, is not lost when the growing child ceases to be a baby or a tot and is called a boy or a girl, and we can count on the fact that he or she will continue to use it in entering on new tasks. But the accumulated learnings and the cumulative effect of learning may make some of the elements under study less visible than they were in early childhood.

Part II
Of Boys and Girls

As a very young child each of us may have studied the action of throwing and discovered that energy must be directed to the hand to hold an object and then to maintain it between the fingers or hands for a while until the appropriate part of the somatic structure can, with a certain additional expenditure of energy, guarantee a throw. The child can perceive the effect of the act at the same time as he notes the act's relationship to the energy expended. Children may also examine whether certain objects have properties that make some throws appear to be more effective than others. They may try to throw a feather or a page of newspaper and compare it with throwing a slipper or a fork.

Very young children give a lot of time to such studies and learn a great deal from them. The act of throwing can itself become a subject of attention, resulting in improvements. But it is left for a more competent child a few years later to notice that perhaps the amount of energy required for a particular throw can be found <u>a priori</u> through a "perceptive" judgment. This kind of study is made by boys and girls under specific circumstances, including the game of marbles (or an equivalent throwing game) and the game of hopscotch (or an equivalent).

We study marbles and hopscotch in this chapter because they are excellent examples of how boys and girls spontaneously educate themselves thoroughly once and for all, putting their perception in the service of action.

No child is allowed to enter a game of marbles to play with other children unless he or she is qualified by the level of his or her performance. This is the reason we see children stratifying themselves in teams of more or less equal competence and entering a game with a fair chance of improving themselves and winning sometimes.

Beginners at the game of marbles give themselves rules which establish the challenge. Usually, one or more marbles are placed on a flat piece of ground, a line is drawn a certain distance from the marbles, and from this line the players throw their own marbles, one at a time. If, after a throw, the distance between a stationary marble and the one just thrown is within an agreed measure (usually a span of a child's hand or length of its foot), the thrower takes away his marble together with the one within the agreed distance. If not, he loses his marble to his opponent.

Clearly, the appearance is that a throw is made in a particular direction to achieve a particular distance. The rule gives a win to the player in precisely defined circumstances. But the reality is that the judgment of the thrower's eye must assess the energy to be put into the throwing apparatus to achieve a perceived end. There is a game because there is an education in it and an inner challenge to the players.

The rules and the appearance of the game are altered as the skills of the players increase, to provide a stiffer and stiffer measure in which the judgment of the energy required for a more precise throw is subordinated to the perceptual judgment of the exact location of the target found by sight.

People find the game engaging precisely because its rules offer a new and more rewarding challenge every time a stage of mastery has been reached. From holding a marble between the thumb and the index finger in the beginning, players end up holding it in a cup formed by the rounded forefinger on the side and the thumb at the bottom. The marble now has to be catapulted by the thumb acting as a spring, while the whole hand and the forefinger give the required orientation for a "carambol" between this marble and one of several others accumulated in a given triangle on the ground. A winner takes the one or more marbles hit out of the triangle, and his own marble as well.

Hence, in moving from an easygoing, informal throw (which allows certain degrees of tolerance, such as bending one's body forward and winning even when a hit is not made) to a strictly erect throw with a special formation of the hand, followed by a direct hit on one or more marbles placed in a restricted space a certain distance away, we have defined an evolution of action. This entails a double movement, a movement of the mind and a movement of the soma: an assessment of the quantity of energy that needs to be mobilized in specific muscles, informed by the explicit judgment from one's sight that objects are at certain distances.

Naturally, one also has to learn to instruct one's wrist to take and hold a certain position with respect to the arm and hand so as to obtain the needed direction for the projectile. The complex behavior is now integrated, and arm, forearm, wrist, hand, and thumb all work as one weapon capable of sending a projectile to a target because of all the computed operations that link the target to the position of the projectile. A hit represents a feedback of correct integration; otherwise, corrections at the firing line must be made to improve accuracy.

Since months of playing are needed to reach this mastery, and since one has rivals most of the time, other components accompany the game, which some observers may consider to be its aim. Collecting marble, trading coveted objects for specially-coveted marbles, fixing one's mind on the ambition to beat a certain player who seems to know how to win every time — even entertaining magic to make oneself invincible — and other components of the continuing involvement can be singled out for examination. Without reducing the importance of these components, we maintain here that the game of marbles is also one of the means chosen to educate children everywhere on our planet in the integration of perception with a complex activity.

What has been learned in this game will be transferred through other games to different kinds of challenges. Using a rubber ball the size of a tennis ball, children play at hitting others who provide a moving target. In baseball the hitter reverses the learning and adjusts his batting to the arriving ball, whose energy, direction, and spin he must surmise and meet with sufficient concentrated energy to place it out of reach of fielders. The pitcher has a role similar to the thrower in the game of marbles and uses that training if it is available.

In archery the lessons learned in games like marbles serve to cut short the adaptation to a new form of throwing. Passing, in American or English football, again shows the transfer of a skill acquired in the game of marbles.

Part II
Of Boys and Girls

While boys mainly play marbles to study how perception can serve action, girls mainly prefer hopscotch, found in many parts of the world. (Today, perhaps, this specialization is no longer as scrupulously observed as in past decades.)

In the game of hopscotch, the players take turns at throwing a small, generally flat stone on a diagram drawn on the ground. Various diagrams are offered to different players according to their level of skills. The rules not only cover the throws, determining the order of successive placements of successful throw (with penalties in the improbable, but not infrequent, landing of the stone on a line or outside the squares), they also add difficulties by allotting players a "house" each time they complete a full turn of throwing and hopping. Each player must hop over anyone else's house in order not to be disqualified.

This additional rule distinguishes hopscotch from the game of marbles and blurs the observation that perception is serving action in this game. But because it is a game of throwing, and because each step is started with a throw, no one can take the game through a number of drawn diagrams involving harder and harder challenges unless the act of throwing is worked on and brought to a certain level of excellence. The stone is not required to hit anything, but the players have to work on their wrists, their hands, and their bodies in order to determine exactly the angle of throw and the energy to be spent to secure the successive placements.

Both hopscotch and marbles illustrate the awareness that one's eyes do not throw, and that the coordination of one's eyes so as

9 Perception at the Service of Action: Marbles and Hopscotch

to produce a complex eye-arm-hand functioning gives sight to one's hand and control over muscular energy to one's eyes. In these two games, it is perception that plays the role of guide, that serves action.

We shall continue our exploration of games in a later chapter. Now, we shall see how action serves perception.

10 Action at the Service of Perception: Why Children Draw

A consistent observation made by students of children of elementary school age is that although almost all children spontaneously get involved in drawing, almost all drop drawing as a form of expression between the ages of eight and ten.

All over the world collections of children's art have displayed, amid cultural differences, a universality that can be due only to a universal function found in the act of drawing — a function summed up in the title of this chapter.

Seeing is synthetic, and the self is aware of global impressions. So long as an overall impression is sufficient for the activities of living and learning in other areas, the self proposes no special exercises to itself. But because classes of impressions are being formed all the time — when the light that falls on a scene changes, when the distances from which objects are seen change, when the angles from which one sees them change — the self is made aware that the analytic powers of the mind can operate through focusing, stressing, and ignoring operations that are available from very early in life.

Any child provided with a box of colored chalks or crayons or paints can readily find a solitary game which does not need verbalization — but is compatible with it — when she or he discovers that color can be placed on a surface (a wall or furniture as well as paper or cardboard) and then places it there deliberately. The result of this activity is that an initiative of the self, known as an action because it involves the expenditure of muscular energy, leads to a perceptible creation. The result was indeed not there before the action. That particular action produced that particular result which can now strike the sight and suggest its own variations.

Actions with coloring stuffs produce perceptibly different results, and new awarenesses may follow: some results are pleasing, some are not. What ways of placing colors near each other produce jarring or agreeable impacts? What effects result from the relative amount of space on a given sheet that is devoted to this or that color? Which colors merge and which give a muddy effect? What changes regularly result from mixing some colors, such as blues with yellows or reds with blues? What effects follow from surrounding some colors by others in various patterns?

All this is open to children to explore with the tools of color and a surface. Not all the possibilities are taken up by everybody. Sometimes economic considerations prevent children from getting the tools, sometimes teachers or parents do not

10 Action at the Service of Perception: Why Children Draw

appreciate the education that follows from this spontaneous search and force children instead to color pictures in books, or to produce patterns by folding sheets on which a few colors have been spread.

But color is only one of the opportunities for action to serve perception. Drawing is another.

Drawings are spontaneous actions which make children practice holding a pencil so that it obeys commands from the self. This coordination of sight and muscle is certainly not the aim of children's drawing nor its motivation. It is a by-product, obtained in passing, but it serves all the activities that require that skill.

In the beginning drawing is used by every child to provide himself or herself with evidence that his consciousness is involved in seeing, and in seeing more analytically. On the whole, there is no need to change the topic or theme of successive drawings to undertake the job of conscious seeing. Most children find enough variety in the same source of inspiration, most frequently human beings and houses.

For the human figure, the body-image is the receptacle of a very complex awareness already explored when learning, for instance, how to put something in one's mouth, or how to judge which part of one's body is assailed by a mosquito or a fly. It is not the outer world that motivates drawing. We find children drawing figures so similar to the impression they make on our trained sight that we can only say that children draw themselves before they draw other people.

Using very scanty outlines, children can draw a believable receptacle endowed with the awareness that it resembles something of themselves, say, their head, rendered by a closed line. Once they know that the circle they have put down divides the plane into two complementary spaces, and when they decide to draw two smaller circles to represent the eyes, they confidently and universally place them inside what we recognize as the interior of the first drawing.

This choice of the inside of the circle by all children cannot result from a topological intuition of the geometrical plane, for some children could have erroneously tried to place the eyes outside at first and then found topological criteria from their perception of faces. Children who have no one they must please by this activity, are aware from inside themselves of the position of their eyes in their face because, for years, they have ordered certain voluntary muscles to contract or relax.

Moreover, when the mouth is added as a third circle inside the outline of the head, it is never placed directly between the eyes but distinctly lower (in an oriented drawing), at least after the first drawing.

Many children do not relate to their nose in the way they show they relate to their eyes and mouth. Sometimes months elapse before they notice that they have left out the nose in their drawing of a face.

The content of each drawing tells two things about perception:

1. that an overall awareness of detail exists, and
2. that a special question is being investigated.

But by what it omits it also says how far the analytic seeing has yet to go to be compatible with the synthetic and to be sufficient for most activities of that age.

Since there is so much to know analytically in a face or a house, many drawings will be produced, each devoted to a particular question. And there are many different questions, about position, location, relative size, texture, color, the relative relationship of elements to each other, and other matters. When one adds that garments are known to be distinct from a figure and can be put on and taken off, the child's consideration of clothes will result in a new set of challenges. Not all trials present acceptable solutions to any of the above questions, and there may be a number of attempts, making it clearer to investigators what a child is doing with this or that particular drawing.

When color, approval or disapproval by people in the environment, and an aesthetic feeling are added, much will be found in any drawing that can divert us from grasping its role in providing the criteria that ensure that conscious seeing has taken place.

Later, when young people are taught perspective, the new draftsmen will integrate a mental attitude with their sight and prove once more that drawing is a way of knowing sight as a mental instrument of the self, that sight is not an organ anatomically and physiologically endowed to see everything all at once.

There is much more to be said about drawing. But first we need to be clearer about the powers that are available to the young people we are considering.

11 Imagery, Virtuality, Symbolism: Extending the World of Action

We set out to find the new tasks which boys and girls, generally between the ages of five or six and ten or eleven, consider to be vital, once they have given themselves to the tasks that ensure their survival in their natural and social environments.

When we examine the ways that were open to mankind to extend its grasp of things, we find that it developed mental powers that tend to reduce the energy cost of action. These innovations were not arbitrary. Men had to respect the reality of action, and they had to generate substitutes that could be combined with the aspects of action that they did not know how to replace. For example, when the lever was proposed as a substitute for the arm in moving large rocks, its appearance and its use remained connected with those of the arm. Although there was no saving of energy as such, Man gave himself the means to tackle some tasks that had earlier been beyond him.

The power of the mind that sees a branch as a lever and an extension for an arm is called imagination. This is a power that all children have. All children demonstrate that what they become aware of during their waking hours can visit them again in their sleep through dreams that seem to have all the properties of reality. Because the functioning of the sense organs is known from inside, the generation of images is everyone's birthright. But only those who become aware of it as a power of the mind will see that it can be used to amplify actions.

Before we call for the help of other hands to pull on a rope, we must know that forces are additive, and we must have seen where to place people so that the resultant pull is greater than that of each person. The period of anyone's experimentation in this field now is normally a great deal shorter than the time it took the original inventors to conceive of it. This is precisely because the gift of imagery can act upon images at a very low cost in mental energy. Through the connection of images to muscles, the correctness of a proposal can be tested virtually — in the mind. The education of mankind in the use of labor-saving devices has always taken very little time once the devices were conceived, just because man's mind can recognize the identity between the dynamics of imagery and the dynamics of actions.

A great deal of time is spent by children of elementary school age in exploring spontaneously the relation between the virtual and the actual, imagination and action. While the contents of this activity will for most of them be removed during adolescence, the know-hows will remain in the form of mental

11 Imagery, Virtuality, Symbolism: Extending the World of Action

dynamics available for work on any content, particularly on thought and systems of symbols.

Speech is already available and is a very good example of virtual functioning that remains in contact with actuality. Words are neither thoughts nor symbols, they are only arbitrary sounds. But they are connected in an intimate manner to meanings. That is, images or emotions or feelings, or several of these are linked to virtual actions and mental dynamics. Words are "triggers" of meanings and, hence, partake of the dynamics of the virtual.

Considering the complex intermingling of actual actions with virtual actions, we can see that life at this period is concerned with vital experiences. Superficially, it may seem that people could do without the "luxury" of symbolism. In man's awareness of himself as a creature able to extend actions to the realm of the virtual, symbolism becomes man's characteristic. Far from being a luxury, it is in symbolism that he will find his fulfillment as man, a tool with which he creates a world of extended actions.

Boys and girls do not discuss this matter as we are doing here. They live it, and so intensely that for us to ignore this profound involvement in images is to miss altogether the meaning of life between five or six and ten or eleven, and, of course, to miss what follows from this total involvement.

Toys are part of the equipment used by boys and girls to superimpose on the world of perception and actions — the true world of their age — a world of extended actions, the unlimited action of a world obeying the mind.

Toys made by children answer their inner needs better than ready-made toys. A toy which is not structured once and for all, as a car or a doll is, is cherished more and used longer. Boys ask for more and more cars, girls for more and more dolls. But they use what I call "multivalent" toys for years, simply by acting upon them to change them into what they want.

While a box can be used as a police car or an ambulance, the ready-made police car is that and only that; hence, the request for more and more cars to meet the power of the imagination in contact with the unchangeable given. While a sheet hanging down from a table turns the space underneath into the kingdom of a child where he or she can act out what he or she fancies, a furnished doll's house imposes its shape and its furniture (although it too can be used symbolically). A stick can become a horse that is ridden around the house as the tongue makes noises evocative of the sound of horses upon cobblestones. The same stick is a sword or a lance or a rifle, or even a machine gun, to be used in imaginary battles with enemies in any numbers, from any group or nation, on any soil, all supplied by a fertile imagination.

In the minds of boys and girls virtual universes are put together in which the self can dwell as it pleases, dominating them and knowing intimately what is possible within them.

We shall have many opportunities to illustrate the above statement from daily occurrences in the lives of elementary school boys and girls. Here we want to look more closely at the power that symbolism gives.

11 Imagery, Virtuality, Symbolism: Extending the World of Action

The extremely matter-of-fact living that goes with a total immersion in the world of action has drawn observers' attention to the appearances rather than to the invisible reality; perhaps both have been missed. The self that is in intimate contact with what goes on in the bag — day and night every hour, alerted to what is new, recasting the old through the effect of new awarenesses, knowing what one has become so that one enters well-equipped into the expanded universe which opens up — this self does not miss its opportunities, even though it does not attempt to share its secrets.

And we do not see that for much of this period living is a kind of dreaming, where the actual is modified by the presence of the flexible and extendable realm of the virtual.

As soon as some content of consciousness gains "virtuality" it becomes a symbol. It becomes an instrument to conquer what needs little time and little energy but can fill the spiritual space available.

Here I can be hero of the kind I want to be. I can transform the world by talking to my pet rabbit. I can affect people's thoughts about me by forcing them to admire what I can become, and have become, instantaneously. See how I jump from building to building in pursuit of a robber, or from tall tree to tall tree to save the victim of a wild beast. Zorro and Tarzan only make visible what I have done a thousand times and confirm the realism of my dream.

Part II
Of Boys and Girls

Cartoons exemplify for me the availability of a process which can change printed figures or symbols into a flow of mental energy that vitalizes me.

The symbols that entertain me and that I entertain are simply those which are compatible with actions and their extensions. They may gain other meanings through the interventions of my older companions at home or at play who see new opportunities in them, such as being a "magnanimous" hero in battles, or being "just" once a victory is assured, or being "generous" after a treasure has been rescued from pirates, and so on.

Living the dream is in no way living the unreal. On the contrary, it is the way the self finds to give full humanity to itself at this age. From the moment of conception, this self knows its part in creating the real and has not yet been fooled be verbal arguments according to the laws of some restrictive logic. This self cannot deny to itself that action has many possibilities but not all; that action is the source of the awareness that virtuality exists and that virtuality widens action by association with it; that virtuality is power.

If a stick can become a horse, cannot the thunder become a warning from a God who — like the sun, which is everywhere and illumines most corners — is intimately mixed up with everybody's life?

Reality for man is inhabited by his many creations, and every generation enters reality without criteria for knowing what is

11 Imagery, Virtuality, Symbolism: Extending the World of Action

man-made or God-made or Nature-made. The environment is not co-extensive with reality, and each individual has his or her experience to testify to what is real and what is not, and each makes some reconciliation between his own inner life and the life of the rest of the universe as he assumes it to be.

We are as susceptible to being taught by legends and stories as we are by facts. We carry in our bag loads of symbols knitted into the fabric of our spiritual substance. We rarely wish to be, or can be, wholly factual. We constantly use metaphors, similes, and analogies to evoke in others to what has meaning for us.

These are some of the dividends that come from owning a source of symbols and a capacity to renew them when we meet new circumstances. When we relate to other people's symbols, we find that they grow on us, that we discover different meanings every time we yield to them, that we can increase our own stock of symbols by adopting those of others.

Symbolism for each individual and symbolism for humanity not only have a different content but are two different processes. The first is alive and at work in each of us. The second is an abstraction, the sum total of all the symbolisms of individuals past and future. Because they are the symbolisms of individuals any individual has an entry into them, can assimilate some of them, and can make them alive for those in the next generations who care to take them.

Part II
Of Boys and Girls

Childhood is so susceptible to symbolism because it is the age that makes the machine that produces symbols through its awareness of virtuality.

12 Finesse and Balance: Jump Rope and Other Games of Energy

There is certainly a great deal to learn about oneself as a system endowed with muscles and a skeleton, with inner perceptions about the ways energy can be used to affect the functioning of muscles and produce physical behaviors that are recognizably new and can link one's soma more intimately with some of the attributes of the outside world.

It is during this time of childhood that we spin ourselves around our spinal axis until dizzy, that we climb trees and swing on branches, that we try to ricochet a stone on the surface of water, that we learn in no time to ride a bicycle, to skate with rollers or on ice, to slide down a banister rather than walk down the stairs, to climb stairs by twos or threes, to go up a down escalator to the annoyance of other users.

How easily motivated we were at that age to enter into games whose functions were to control the amount of energy manifested through one's foot, shifting our weight from one foot to another in going from one square to the next on a diagram drawn on the ground! How many different games we invented when we had the use of a rope!

A number of these games educate an important awareness we call "finesse."

For a child who knows how to lift herself from the ground, jump rope is the opportunity to study how to delegate the right amount of energy to the legs to produce a rhythmic movement coordinated with the rhythmic movements of a rope controlled by the hands. The challenge to the arms is soon mastered and produces the framework for transferring attention to the legs and feet, although attention is returned to the hands when increased speed is required. The game requires one to increase the number of successive jumps and thus provides a feedback-count to measure the improvement resulting from practice.

For boys and girls, jump rope is "the" way of knowing and educating the awareness of changes of energy in relation to the functioning of the legs when jumping. Months and months are needed to ensure mastery of the dynamics. As long as mastery has not been reached, the rope is a source of excitement, of enthusiasm, and an immediate invitation to get on with the jumping.

12 Finesse and Balance: Jump Rope and Other Games of Energy

The game does not require the solitary player to make thousands of jumps without interruption. This component only appears when the game becomes competitive and involves a group of players or a rope manned by two people. Boxers jump rope for another purpose, as an indicator of endurance, and may well want to go on to a count of thousands of jumps.

A rope has little appeal at first unless one sees other children jumping with it and generating contagion through it. A boy or girl given a rope knows how to jump in a number of ways but is baffled by the division of attention required to turn the rope from back to front using the wrists and arms, and the concomitant effort to lift the feet from the ground at the moment just before the rope reaches the feet.

A number of mistakes in the beginning are enough for the self to know that there is plenty of time to shift attention from hands to legs, to give previously programmed orders to get both working, and then to subordinate a simple rhythm (that of the hands) to the harder one (that of the legs, since the whole body has to be lifted).

In fact, most children master this coordination on the first day. But then the question of practice — which ensures the repetition of the same succession of commands — changes itself into the exploration of what is compatible with the temporal gestalt of the person who is skipping. The initiative is the child's. He or she can speed up the rotation of the arms and at the same time order the feet to leave the ground at the swifter pace imposed by the turning rope. He or she can separate the orders given to the two feet so that they do not leave the ground together, but one after the other, although sufficiently close together to fit two movements of the legs into the time of one quick turn of the rope. He or she can try to walk while skipping and even to hop on one leg while the rope is turning.

Would it be a game if there were no successive broadening of the challenges, each proving that the previous one had been mastered and was available to be taken on to the next?

When two players have one rope and decide to jump together, one of them must turn the rope, already knowing how to adjust his or her jumps to its rhythm, while the second one has to sense what is right from seeing the shoulders or eyes of the playmate go up and down and make the jumps accordingly. When a number of players take a turn in a rope game where two people are turning the rope, there is a challenge in entering and jumping at the right times rather than being caught by the flying rope and hurt.

Even if the children do not express their experience as an education and their play as hard work spent in reaching a knowledge of themselves as somatic systems engaged in disciplined activities that yield specific improvements of functionings, there are modalities in this game which allow us to say it on their behalf. Not only are there increased challenges in the number of jumps which express good performance, in the speed of jumping which may be coupled with a large number of jumps, in changing the speed of rotation or alternating different speeds without warning, in allowing two players to enter a

12 Finesse and Balance: Jump Rope and Other Games of Energy

turning rope from opposite directions; there are also systematic exercises to prepare for each of these, which occupy the minds of the players night and day. The total immersion when this game is prevalent, especially in the case of girls, feeds back to the self the information that the discipline is accepted, that the tasks are serious and important, that the expansion of the self which accompanies the activities when they are well done, are all signs that one has refined oneself in this field.

When the game is over for good, the players have almost no memory of the sessions or the time they spent. The brand of memory built in the soma is the improved use of oneself, the availability of skillful muscular patterns stored in the mind and its imagination. The absence for most of us of anecdotal memory about the game tells us that most people do not jump rope as a social function but in order to achieve better awareness of their use of their soma. Because these games are active, the gains they represent are inscribed in the ways the self manifests itself in its somatic behaviors.

Of course, the choice of games with a rope is only one among many which provide children of this age with finer uses of themselves and allow them to explore integrated mental-somatic actions. On a swing the younger child expects the impulse to come from outsiders; the older child discovers how to use the combination of gravitational energy and the energy that results from varying the distribution of the limbs, trunk, and head within the system. Besides a gratifying feeling of independence and autonomy, the newly acquired techniques tell the child on the swing that he can give himself to the activity as long as he wants and vary as much as he wishes the height attained and the speed of swinging.

At the same time as they study the fine characteristics of their active selves, most children deliberately conquer balance. If a boy is given a bicycle, he will soon learn to ride it and begin to study whether he can ride without touching the handlebars, or with only the lightest touch of a finger. He will, one day, much later, attempt acrobatics on the bicycle, but if they require too much energy, he will postpone them until physical bulk is available to him.

There seems to be a fascination in the walls that serve as guards on cliffs, bridges, promenades by the sea. Children, mainly boys, climb them and run along them to the despair of accompanying adults. Walking on imaginary or actual lines on floors or roads, putting one foot in front of the other, balancing with one's arms stretched, blindfolded or not — children of the age we are considering know precisely that they are trying to conquer parts of the world of action. A beam lying on the floor of an abandoned building seems an invitation to test oneself. A number of stepping stones scattered on the bed of a stream is another invitation to jump from one to the other while avoiding a fall.

Because it is the age of action, the surrounding universe is seen as animated by children. There seems to be a dimension to all objects that can become active, and this dimension is gotten hold of by every child. Far from being the expression of the primitive alive in the child, it is the expression rather of the

12 Finesse and Balance: Jump Rope and Other Games of Energy

perceptive person who proves that he is stressing action in everything that is compatible with it.

The overflow of energy at the somatic level makes the child play somatic games for hours every day so that he or she comes to know all the expressions of the soma that we call action. He not only seems never to tire, he is at a low ebb in his somatic vulnerability. A child can take endless beatings from companions and neither cry nor complain. For a boy the mere appearance of a boy his own age seems a provocation to a physical struggle. In such a struggle, because the boy is intimately aware of the extent of muscle and bone resistance, he very rarely turns another's neck too far even though it is captured between his arm and forearm and against his chest. In fact, he knows, from inside, the suppleness of a body to the extent that only acrobats and fakirs do in later years.

Children of this age seem to worship action, and all places where they can come in contact with it become temples sacred to them.

13 Filling the World with Dynamics

What we are trying to do in this section is to restore to boys and girls their right to be met in their acts of living, even if this can be done only in a very limited way in the genre of a scientist rather than a novelist.

The boys and girls who people my mind are not only images, many of them nameless; they come from my own experience as a boy surrounded by boys and girls of my own age, all of us brought to life by our acts of living. What I see in the many boys and girls in the many elementary schools where I have worked is the passionate search for truth as it appears to them in their lives, the dedication to knowing the world (both inner and outer) as far as they can grasp it with instruments available to them. In fact, they are not different from the way I see myself today in my world (inner and outer).

As a boy I was as complete as I am now many decades later. I had not accumulated the experiences of the following years, but

I had days as full as I now have, moments as challenging as today's.

I see the boys and girls as epistemologists, knowing what there is to know and how to achieve it, proceeding as legitimately as Locke or Hume or Kant or anyone else who asked, "What is there to know?" and who embarked on finding a satisfactory answer. The keen minds of boys and girls seize the fact that the world is a world in constant change. There is day and night, changes in the weather, the beginning and the end of many involvements, whether eating a meal or taking a nap. They see themselves grow and become capable of doing what was not possible earlier. They break things and cannot put them together. From all this, they know that the world is a place where things happen, where a few changes are reversible and many irreversible.

They have little interest in anything which has to remain intact, although they teach themselves to respect it in order to stay out of trouble with people capable of interfering with their peace. Whenever they can alter the environment, they do it with delight, so long as it does not represent hard or routine work. Everyone can count on their cooperation if the alteration can be done easily and quickly, but will be disappointed if they expect the volunteers to be around to do the same thing spontaneously again and again.

This is because there are other things to do with one's time, more exciting things, always different for the self aware of its functions, even if, from the outside, the appearance is one of repetition. A learner knows whether mastery has been reached or if there is need for further practice.

What a child sees in a task is his involvement. Observers cannot reach the invisible. They have to assume it and look for evidence of its existence. Seeing a child watch cartoons on TV for five hours at a stretch may lead to a conclusion drawn from his passive presence, but this belies the conception of his active self. Ask the child to watch documentaries or love stories for five hours and at once you will know that this special attention to cartoons is from something sui generis. Tell him that they are uninteresting, stupid, empty, and repetitive to many grownups, and he will protest, "I do not have to find them stupid because you do not like them. They are very interesting to me."

This contained activity in front of the TV set is, in fact, a proof of the capacity of children at this age to endow the slightest mention of action with the whole of themselves. It is this gift that animates their world.

We can easily live at two levels at the same time, particularly if one is virtual and the other actual. Just as we know that once we shut our eyes we can evoke what we were seeing and still know the difference between the evoked image and the seen reality, we know that we are engaged in receiving impacts from the outer world and processing them into mental actions. Only exceptionally do some people suffer the delusion of being concerned with just one world.

Riding a stick, jumping over a wide river which is actually a narrow path or a narrow stream, climbing a mountain while only lifting oneself onto small boulders or rocks, pursuing an entirely imaginary army in defeat — all this is ordinary currency for boys of seven or eight. It is also the way our ordinary world is made worthy of the greatest adventurer.

When a few children come together they must accommodate to each other: the younger ones let the older ones lead. The words that are spoken, the orders that are given, may be filled with different meanings by all of them, but the surrender of the younger ones and the imagination of the older ones blend to provide each with what he can accept at the moment. The older children may place a younger one as a sentry to watch for enemies that may never materialize while they, the older ones, climb to their fortress to prepare for battle, standing on a rock looking down on their obedient sentry and the surrounding fields. The thrill of belonging to an army that has a captain fills the soldier with pride, and he holds himself erect and alert so as to be worthy of his election.

There is nothing in the world that cannot be transformed, and if Don Quixote were a child, there would be nothing strange in his changing sheep into soldiers and windmills into fortresses. Indeed, what Cervantes attributed to the actual suffices to generate all the virtual attributes compatible with it.

Children provide themselves in this way with a dynamic universe holding in its content futures that are indeed pregnant with invisible possibilities.

13 Filling the World with Dynamics

Are not the visionaries in our societies operating in a similar manner, extending the appearances of reality to include what they see to be compatible with them? Is it not much easier to endow a horse with wings and let him gallop over the clouds than to solve all the problems which lead to aviation? Or to take refuge in a whale and explore the deep sea in one's mind than to produce the submarine? The sense of adventure would not be found in adults if the capacity of the minds of children to reduce obstacles through the virtual did not exist universally. The long familiarity with the virtual at this age of childhood leaves its marks on everyone, including pusillanimous and cowardly adults who can only dream acts of courage. The readiness to attempt to open doors that others have found cannot be opened owes its existence to this sense, the sense that "I can do anything" — which is only true in the virtual.

Although the movement of the mind is only in the direction of making the impossible possible, the exploration of the universe of action teaches the limitations of action and leads to a realistic attitude which nevertheless remains tinted with daring, with hope, and with incentive, an attitude that tries to break through the perceived boundaries. We gave ourselves to this education as boys and girls; we end up with a universe susceptible to change that we hope will meet our desires because we continue to see it as a universe that involves us and the workings of our minds. The boy or girl in each of us has given us a dynamic and expanding universe in which to live as spiritual beings.

14 Games: Their Phases, Purposes, and Opportunities

Games, as we already have indicated, are of paramount importance in our lives, and when we are boys and girls they form the most significant part of our days. They are the source of our true education, the one that will remain with us in a multitude of smooth functionings and in an arsenal of enhanced sensitivities leading to deeper and clearer perceptions. They are also the vehicles for additional lessons about ourselves and our human and natural environment.

Boys and girls play many games, mostly games of skill, but also games that explore areas of experience that will matter to them much later. We have already looked at playing marbles, at hopscotch, at games with a rope, which extend over months or even years, and we have seen the special education they provide the players.

Part II
Of Boys and Girls

What strikes the student of spontaneous games is a child's sudden interest in a certain activity and an equally sudden cessation of interest with, in between, a tremendous dedication to the exercises involved — perhaps to the point of losing sleep over them.

Official education has left to these games the job of carrying out informally what perhaps it does not even suspect is part of an individual's education. Parents, who are often baffled by the ease with which their children move from one interest to another, may see their offspring as unsystematic and inconsistent. Teachers who believe that schools are for the transmission of knowledge and culture from one generation to the next do not even suspect that the real education of each of us may be found in the involvement we have in evolving spontaneous games.

Playing spontaneously, apparently for fun, or learning a skill in order to earn one's living, reveal the same structuring of experience. This is no accident. On the contrary, it tells us that learning pervades play and must therefore appear again and again whenever the games change. The aim, whether earning a living or having fun, is secondary or even irrelevant to the temporal sequence that must be adopted to attain the proper use of oneself in the mastery of a functioning.

At any stage in one's evolution in life, one uses oneself to meet the unknown. Large or small questions about the unknown must be met in their character of being unknown, that is, outside one's experience. How else could we meet the unknown than by

14 Games:
Their Phases, Purposes, and Opportunities

being extremely vigilant, cautious, reflecting after each step, being alert to withdraw from a tentative involvement as soon as it proves dangerous?

Again and again every learner at any age sees that during this first phase, which can be called "contact with the unknown," much time is needed for little visible progress. But the feeling that some aspect of the unknown is becoming more familiar, that one's self has passed from not knowing what to do to being engaged in an action that yields at least something, feeds back to the self that the process of learning is on the move.

The first phase may last for minutes or for days. In the case of learning to ride a bicycle, for instance, there are several components to become aware of and to coordinate before one feels comfortable that one is on the saddle and ready to go. It may take many trials if one has to do it all alone, but only a few minutes if someone else can hold the bicycle upright and supply the first push or even the equilibrium of the rider-bicycle system. In the case of learning to jump a rope, where all must be done by oneself, it may take many, many trials just to know how to start jumping. In the case of games of marbles, the phase of learning to hold the marble on one's thumb to push it in a given direction takes quite some time.

It is clear that within a game that has many ramifications and takes a long time to be covered, there are many "first" phases — all the stages when a new skill is suddenly added.

The first phase testifies to the adventurousness of man and his readiness to throw himself into uncharted activities.

Phase two of the apprenticeship is devoted to establishing criteria to test one's level of achievement. This phase is characterized by what we call practice.

The elation accompanying a movement towards mastery is always visible in players who have done well; it also indicates that the self has found what it needs to turn a project into a reality.

The soma changes as a result of all this, although appearances may not change at all. A self with the capacity to skip or hop is not the same as a self without this capacity. Every boy or girl knows this and aims to become more himself or herself by devoting time — the substance of life — to this transformation.

Children need neither persuasion to enter some games nor urging to persist for hours through demanding exercises. The feedback is an inner one, even when an appreciative audience applauds. The inner subtle recognition that a change here or a change there is just what is needed to free a functioning, or to bring in a needed contribution from stored know-hows, keeps the self at work on the components of this field of activity. All this, though invisible to the optical eye, is recognizable by the insight that is activated by feedbacks in the self.

Phase two shows swifter involvements, more complex behaviors, longer stretches of practice, a progressive shifting from concentrating on the thing one has to integrate to being the transformed person who has integrated it.

In learning to ride a bicycle, one may fall, get up at once, remount, go a little further, fall again, get up once more, put oneself on the saddle again, somehow manage to ride much further before falling again, and soon have all this behind one, even forgotten, moving instead towards using the mastery attained to conquer new worlds.

It has not been possible to describe phase two without finding phase three surreptitiously showing its head. In phase three, a mastery of the whole of the new functioning begins to dominate the "local" masteries which tell the self that this or that particular functioning has been achieved.

When this subtle mixture of local and total mastery is replaced by a clear perception that mastery has been achieved, the individual arrives at phase four, and the self utilizes the gains to move to an altogether different involvement.

The hierarchy of games played by boys and girls illustrates this movement. Once all the functionings involved in playing marbles are available to the self, new challenges are perceived. Can we be as good at hitting a moving object as we were at hitting a static target? A soft ball and running playmates are now required, and the game looks very different from the one that preceded it — more so when cunning runners deceive the hitter by turning, running up and down the terrain, hiding behind trees, and so on.

Part II
Of Boys and Girls

A bow and arrow, a target that can be placed as near or as far away as one likes, that is as narrow or as wide as one chooses — all these increasingly difficult challenges suggest seeking further development.

It is possible that, instead of refining the self, so as to create new functionings to take man further on the road to using himself with greater mastery, the target can occupy the mind. Then, instead of games we may have wars and also weapons industries that increase the probability of reaching a target by, say, putting a machine gun at the disposal of the soldier instead of a gun (which has already replaced the bow and arrow). A gun still retains something which reminds us of the role of the self in finding its target and shooting at it. The machine gun works on the probabilities of hits, and increases it chances by increasing the number of "throws" to saturation levels.

The only fun a machine gun offers boys and girls is the noise it makes and the feeling of power that goes with the domination of a situation.

Boys and girls play all sorts of games — from dice and card games that only require one, two, or three players, to team games, such as football, that need many. Because games are the way the self gives itself a spontaneous education, all games that reveal a reachable aspect of the self can be entered into. Of course, no game will be played for long if it only repeats a previous game under another guise.

If chance is an element that catches the interest, then games of chance will be acceptable. But if certainty rather than probability is what needs to be studied, games of chance will be postponed.

If knowing a particular person is of interest, then any game that that person wants to play (including games of chance) will be acceptable.

If learning to be a loser is important, then one enters into games where there are winners and losers to offer oneself an opportunity to contemplate the effects of losing.

If learning to be a leader is significant, then one gets involved in actions which give one the chance to select partners, to organize them within the rules of team operation, and to give oneself the right to change things as one learns by experience.

If learning about strategy is of interest, then activities which offer the opportunity to spend time contemplating it become worthwhile.

If learning about one's imagination or one's creative mental powers becomes important, then specific games that foster these powers become attractive.

Games of chance tell us that the world of boys and girls is ruled by their own "structurations." When they lose games of chance, particularly when they lose a number of times in succession, it becomes proof that they are doomed, that capricious and untraceable invisible forces are at work against them. For a long while, games of chance bring out the worst in children manifested by bad moods and a willingness to spoil a game by leaving it. Later on, vaguely reconciled to the unpredictability of chance, they try to cajole it or to use magic (which seems to be of the same nature) to turn it in their favor. They feel no particular mental discomfort that chance must abandon others to be on their side. Much, much later in life games of chance can be seen for what they are, and the decision to remain in or drop out of the game can be based on an estimation of the odds.

If there is more than one child in a family, and the age difference is no more than three or four years, many games serve the purpose of increasing the acquaintance between the siblings. The opportunity of being together for a stretch of time, involved in apparently the same activity, giving and receiving orders; testing one's imagination against that of the other, one's tolerance of the other, one's cruelty, resistance to being teased, capacity to tease, capacity to restrain oneself, to control one's tears, to refrain from calling on adult assistance against the other — are also motivations for entering into some games. A great deal of psychology can be learned, a great deal about oneself, one's responsiveness to others, one's ability to manipulate, lead, engage, entertain, and so on. The memory of some of these moments lingers, enhancing their significance as educators of the social being in each of us.

In most games, there are no failures, for mistakes are permissible, and penalties remove the sense of guilt. One always learns, perhaps more from mistakes than from straight hits. An awareness of the positive role of mistakes and the value of being confronted with the results of one's actions, whatever they are, is part of the education derived from games.

The loser in a game of chance cannot see any mistake in his actions, yet finds that failure exists. It must be placed on someone else's shoulders, since it was caused not by his own actions but by a mysterious and unfair force just when he expected to do well. Failure results from irrationality, not from the activity.

Games where there is a winner and one or more losers provide an opportunity to gain an education from the mood associated with the outcome — triumphant if one wins, sad and perplexed if one has lost.

A multitude of games have adversaries, rivals, and opponents, forming the teams at play. They make it plain that "we can't win them all" and provide the basis for a view of oneself as a competitor exerting to be the winner or to make the other the loser. Sometimes adversary games lead to the recognition of one's mastery in some use of oneself or of this mastery in another, nourishing a pride in oneself or admiration for the other. These are by-products of the activity.

In games involving many players in two teams, each will need a leader. Boys and girls may value the game as much for the opportunity it gives them to learn to lead and to assess the qualities of leadership in others, as for the activity itself. Sometimes to be the leader on a school ground, one needs only to be there first. As the players arrive, their distribution into two teams is made by one of many methods of choice: "eeny, meeny, miny, mo," for example, or the captains walking towards each other, foot in front of foot, until one treads on the other. A leader, a captain, takes part in the ritual of selection as seriously as in the rest of the game to which it soon belongs. All these devices indicate a shift from the purely content-filled game to a mixed game where social challenges are noted, extracted, and dealt with. Getting into a team can become as much a preoccupation as being a wise leader who selects the fit, the strong, and the swift to be on one's side. Children feel unfairnesses as horrible acts, and if two teams are selected in a process that gives an enormous advantage for one side, the game is neither worth playing nor watching. Two teams that have an equal chance to win are the only acceptable match.

This will not prevent children from giving their enthusiastic allegiance to an adult team that plays to win, that is, to make others lose. This is a different affair. The adulated team operates on an inaccessible plane, whereas the vital games that engages a child serve his or her growth and the growth of the other players.

15 Drawings: Self—Knowledge and the Power of Sight

In Chapter 2, we began to examine why children draw. This activity, in which so many children everywhere engage, has more to tell us of the challenges and tasks that children set themselves.

Let us consciously look at a face and make a list of the items that may require numerous successive drawings by one child who is working on knowing what it is to see all that a face shows.

We can first list the items that one immediately acknowledges as distinct: the face as surface, a boundary between the world and that part of the bag; the two eyes; one nose and two nostrils; one mouth; two ears; a brow; two eyebrows; hair.

Then we note the details of each item: the eyes have eyelids, eyelashes, a pupil, a white part, lacrimal glands; the mouth has lips, teeth; the face has cheeks, a chin, temples, a lever jaw; ears have lobes, convolutions, a rim; a nose has relief, two contours for the nostrils; hair sits on and surrounds the face. Then we see how the placing of each item in the whole requires awareness of relative position and of relative and absolute size.

Finally, there are invisible elements that generate the awareness of relationships, of the blending of the parts, of the resemblance to a human face which may carry any one of the many expressions of emotion, mood, or posture.

Clearly, to investigate all this requires much to be done, and since there is no compulsory order nor a certainty that any problem can be solved in one attempt, many drawings will be needed to cope with errors. There may be errors of choice in attempting to render a particular feature before something else is mastered; errors of solution, which are found to be based on wrong assumptions rather than wrong designs (for example, on flat paper the three-dimensionality of the head must be forgotten and replaced by a device in the drawing itself, and one may assume that ears must be behind the face, so falsifying the proportions); errors in perceiving something that does not belong to the face, such as light and shadow; errors in the rendition (particularly if colors are used) and one does not know whether working on the apparent defect or on something around it will remedy the impression. If we add glasses, hats, scarves, earrings, and makeup to the face, we have need for more trials to take care of it all.

15 Drawings:
Self—Knowledge and the Power of Sight

Such drawings represent a study of oneself in a dialogue with the universe of perception.

Another phase in children's drawing appears when children attempt to analyze movement and another phase when they want to understand action.

These drawings are not studies of visual perception. They are opportunities to objectify the "feel" of oneself in a state of motion: walking, running, climbing, falling, bending, lifting, grasping, holding on. Which muscles are representative of each of these states: legs, back, arms, hands, the whole body? The dialogue this time is between the hand that draws and the mind that is somatically questioning parts of the soma.

Remarkable results can be reached by some of these analysts, who may lack the draftsman's know-how but do not lack an entry into the challenge. Some school-children's drawings have been praised by consummate painters for having achieved without schooling what years of study sometimes cannot make available. The obvious explanation of this paradox is that children dwell in their activity. Their consciousness inhabits their state and lets their self find the transmutations that coordinate their feeling with their will and the instruments they have available.

Similarly, one finds that other problems of composing a picture containing multitudes of figures, such as enemy battalions meeting on a battlefield, does not seem to deter the young draftsman who gets on with his job and places his soldiers here and there, his cannon, his trenches, trees, fortifications, flags, and reserves. Once the drawing is done, it is abandoned as if it were soiled paper. Sartre's statement that "the artist is more precious than his work," because the artist can produce more works with equal ease, applies to such children, and they seem to know it. Another occasion, another piece of paper, a little time, and another battle will be enacted.

These frescoes may become more realistic when the laws of perspective are taught at school. But even without perspective, the spatial arrangement, the position of the various armies and the weapons, the angles of the bodies, are all testimony to a mind full of consciousness of what makes action and how to display it on any scale.

We can say about perspective that its discovery is not a necessity, and indeed it was not discovered by many civilizations that lasted for centuries. It was found and first used by Italian Renaissance painters and then taught to every aspiring artist. It has since been universally used by painters except when the cubists and other abstractionists have questioned its dominance. Children who have lived with action have ample experience that the distortions which result from a particular viewpoint are illusory; they know that the small becomes large when we come near it and the large gets small when we are far from it. The image can be corrected in the mind through knowledge supported by evidence.

Our eye, which we have educated for years, can be educated again at any stage, and when we become acquainted with the rules of perspective, we can produce images that take it into account. We use thought to give images a flexibility, which makes it possible to recognize that a drawing transforms what we have perceived rather than catalogues our perceptions. Practice in using perspective gives us an eye that sees it in the environment as realistically as it sees colors or shapes. However, the mind transcends this modification of the image and can reach new transformations that may affect the image very differently. For example, it can conceive of counter-perspective and of mixing primitive, cubist, and realistic images.

The boys and girls we have been looking at through their work are not investing in the future, they are using some available instruments to reach self-knowledge, a self-knowledge that is concerned with the analytic powers of their minds in relation to the overall synthetic power of sight. The self-knowledge is not an end in itself; it becomes yet another instrument with which to dominate the environment and to master some relationships with it.

In some societies, such an education was considered necessary for coping with challenges and dangers, and was seen as something demanded by life, something essentially biological. In modern urban societies, it is only a short phase of one's life, and most people do not regret not having become painters. Most people do not even suspect that they gave themselves such an education and that they hold a gift they can use to give themselves satisfaction and enjoyment.

16 Partnerships: The Necessary Selfishness of Children

Anyone who has seen children of elementary school age change schools, or move from one area to another, has noticed the ease with which links with school friends or neighbors and constant companions are forgotten. It seems that emotional and sentimental connections are not for this age. And this attitude is in agreement with the major stress on action.

What we consider most seriously when we are adolescents is barely a matter of attention now, for all the dialogues at this age are with the self involved in activities that mainly require an egocentric attitude. Skills demand concentration on the task and a reduction of any distractions. Hence, there is no real demand for anything beyond a momentary linkage to others, and then only as long as the linkage serves the end in mind. In the period preceding adolescence, and more so the further away from it, boys and girls know how to use others for their own ends. This is not done as a deliberate exploitation of others; it is in fact a partnership where each partner uses the other.

So long as a partner is needed to achieve an investigation that the self recognizes as vital, the partner is welcomed and involved as an alter ago in the investigation. The appearance is one of a solid friendship based on common interest and mutual benefit as well as on delight in each other. But beware! The slightest infringement by one of the partners on the expectations of the other causes everything to break down. The broken rule seems so much more important than the friendship that the friend of a minute ago becomes a villain with whom no intercourse is now possible. Sometimes a ritual formalizes the break; for example, two crossed fingers of one partner are separated by a finger of the other. After such rituals, each will look for another partner to pursue the vital game, ready to break the new friendship if it is as unsatisfactory as the first, and so on.

Of course, since feelings are high at the time, and the reasons that generated the indignation are not very deep, a broken friendship often is mended. Nevertheless, the links are essentially fragile, and no one truly attempts to make them stronger. They are subordinated to the function of the partnership, which is the selfish growth of the partners engaged in the activities of the time, which often cannot be undertaken by oneself alone.

If by chance rules are not broken, and more and more games that involve more than one person are completed to the satisfaction of the partners, a lasting friendship may result, one

16 Partnerships:
The Necessary Selfishness of Children

that continues through adolescence to become a friendship for life. But how many of us have had them, or have even heard of them?

Boys and girls are not yet gregarious and do not go out of their way to belong to a gang, but they know very well that for some activities and some games they have to team up with others to make the thing work. Pragmatically, they form groups to play hide-and-seek, to leapfrog, to play card games, to do some acting, to be in any one of the hundreds of games where one's mastery of the activity requires competitors or associates or arbiters.

Some of the time they learn that something about the behavior of their peers or other children is obvious but incidental, and there are so many occasions where they seem not to be learning much about social intercourse that this cannot be fortuitous. Since children at this age are devoted to the study of action, the social forms which are compatible with this study will be entertained, will take form, take root. But others will be noticed only if something striking accompanies them and many will not reach consciousness clearly and will be ignored.

Insofar as they are routine, the rules of life in a family are observed, and parents find this age far less demanding than earlier or later ones. So long as children are left alone to play with their toys, they will not ask for attention. So long as they can watch their murder stories on TV, they will be no trouble. Since they neither have opinions on matters discussed on political, economic, or social levels, have no personal needs beyond the purchase of some toys or some materials to make things for certain purposes, they do not attempt to enter into transactions for money as they will do later.

They are, of course, ready to give up a small amount of time to chores which are not too difficult in exchange for some consideration and some peace to play their vital games. They take for granted that they belong to a family, but do not give it the blind loyalty of adolescents. Generally, boys and girls remain at home (unless they are the victims of conditions of antagonism) because they are not yet moved to look at their home critically. Their fertile imaginations make real conditions, whether of poverty or cleanliness or tidiness, less noticeable, supplying factors which embellish the space. Rats and cockroaches, lizards and ants are no more than nuisances.

They do not mind having to wear a torn or inelegant garment; neither do they think that overmuch washing is good for them. What matters is that they have a place, a social place where they can do what they want to do. Society is all right so long as it leaves them alone and does not ask them to do much more than take care of themselves on their own terms.

On the one hand, they show great indifference towards what is transcendental and, on the other, extreme vulnerability to the observance of rules and rituals in games, making them intolerant, vindictive, and even cruel.

This description of boys and girls bears considerable resemblance to certain adult societies where most members of

16 Partnerships: The Necessary Selfishness of Children

the group have a sensitivity to what touches their interest coupled with a total indifference to what concerns others, making so many evil group behaviors possible.

Elementary school boys and girls do not question the fact that they belong to this family, this community, this state, this country. It is part of the given that they have no desire to change. There is enough for them to do to know the environment as a fact, perhaps an eternal fact that may have been there from the beginning of the world — that is, with their coming into it.

Indeed, how can one want to change one's environment if one does not yet know it or know a different one? First, then, one devotes one's time to assimilating the environment and has a lot of fun doing it because of the expansion of oneself that goes with it. Much later, when one's mind is furnished with this and other actual or imagined realities, one thinks of altering the aspects of the environment that strike one as changeable. If enthusiasm for social action can be created in boys and girls, it is generally short-lived, and even then it is the content <u>per se</u> that mobilizes them. Cleaning one's street can be fun, once, if many people get involved, if things are visibly moved. But cleaning one's street every day is of no interest to them because it has no meaning in the vital work they require to do for themselves.

Permanent groupings beyond the family to not attract them, and if groups are formed in a street or a building, the reasons for staying together escape them and are capable of breaking down at the slightest provocation. Brothers and sisters, cousins and neighbors, fight with each other all the time, not through malice or hatred, not even dislike, but because each situation is an opportunity to know one as a teaser, a victim, a skilled fighter, as capable of obtaining favors from others, of being protected by others, of exploring the harmlessness of some acts and the dangers of others. Brothers and sisters so often give the impression of being enemies, ready to jump at each other's throat, threatening each other with eternal disowning, but they soon join to exploit each other in a game both want to play and cannot play without the other.

Boys and girls who are so knowledgeable in the field of action pay the price of being deprived of criteria in the fields where their elders are consciously living. They therefore have to guess much of the meaning of social intercourse and are more often wrong than right in their guesses.

Since they have developed a more liberal sense of property than they had in their first years and do not need to own static objects in order to know them as they did then, they pay far less attention to who owns what and can unthinkingly take someone else's property. This makes them delinquent in the eyes of the adults, but they have no sense of guilt, as they will in later years, since there was no inner participation in the act.

Objects have functions for them as people do . Just as boys and girls can drop h other with eternal disowning, but they soon join to exploit each other in a game both want to play and cannot play without the other.

16 Partnerships:
The Necessary Selfishness of Children

Boys and girls who are so knowledgeable in the field of action pay the price of being deprived of criteria in the fields where their elders are consciously living. They therefore have to guess much of the meaning of social intercourse and are more often wrong than right in their guesses.

Since they have developed a more liberal sense of property than they had in their first years and do not need to own static objects in order to know them as they did then, they pay far less attention to who owns what and can unthinkingly take someone else's property. This makes them delinquent in the eyes of the adults, but they have no sense of guilt, as they will in later years, since there was no inner participation in the act.

Objects have functions for them as people do the destruction of a piece of furniture or windows or any other object, they put their whole self into the activity.

Adults are baffled by the thoroughness of the destruction; children are baffled by the reference to elements such as cost, public ownership or ugliness, which are transcendental and hence invisible. When Rousseau suggested teaching Emile the consequences of breaking windows by letting him catch a cold, he was telling us not only that lessons of direct perception are right for children of that age but also, indirectly, that he did not have a very good solution for vandalism: pneumonia and death are not equivalent to a pane of glass. One of the most influential thinkers in education could not understand that boys and girls, like all of us, live at their own level of awareness and must be met there. No one can insert into a boy's consciousness the recognition that some actions which do not present any danger to him are reprehensible, or that he should stick to his partners even when these do not seem to perform their function in the partnership.

In this chapter we have tried to understand why the involvement in action permits only some aspects of life to reach the mind and blocks others, and we have met the constant factor of awareness, which is always awareness of something definite until awareness of one's awareness becomes one's lot. This development tends not to happen before mid-adolescence and, even if it happens, it does not seem to remain with everyone.

There are so many jobs asking for the total attention of the children we are looking at that we must not be surprised that many other jobs are neglected and escape awareness. Children are not protected from, or even warned about, these matters, and in this area lies the dangers of misunderstanding that can occur between members of the same group with different ages.

If children do not understand adults, the converse is also true.

17 Equity and Morality: The Ethic of Action

In our study of boys and girls, we also have opportunities to study mankind when we consider fundamental questions. The psychological foundations of morality is one such question.

Because several generations live simultaneously on Earth there seems to be a movement of knowledge (of any kind) from the older generations to the younger. However, in most fields we must learn from scratch, all of us, and prepare ourselves to take responsibility for our actions. The experience of others serves us little, and when it does, it is in specific ways for which we also need preparation.

Morality is no exception to this general rule: we generally must learn it from scratch.

For the person who is absorbed in the study of some vital component in life, anything the person meets that is related to this component is accessible at once. Relevance comes from the capacity of awareness to dwell in what is met. Children who are involved in an activity therefore develop at the same time a capacity to assess the world as a respondent to their needs of the moment. Within this general frame of reference two distorting factors appear: one that makes us ignore much that is connected with what we are involved in and one that makes us exalt the relevance to the perceived situation of what we do see.

Since what we do not perceive does not touch us, we almost never move in advance to prevent ills or evils from suddenly falling on us. Our ethical mechanisms, like our sensory ones, are moved by impacts. Hence, we cannot be surprised to find boys and girls operating morally in a manner that is subordinated to their perception of themselves in the world. As mentioned in the previous chapter, the consequences of their actions often seem entirely out of proportion to boys and girls, since they had no intention other than performing those actions. The powers of society do not "react" to children's actions in the sense this word has in physics; instead, society seems to take initiatives that are unrelated to the action and to endow the actor with elements that he or she knows are non-existent.

Indignation is a feeling that each of us knows almost from the beginning of life. It operates automatically in most of us as a "reaction" when we perceive that we are not being equitably taken into account.

Pulling away food from a baby who is still feeding generates indignation which subsides only when the food is returned and the function is restored. Confiscating toys from school children

17 Equity and Morality:
The Ethic of Action

likewise creates indignation. The difference between the two ages in the handling of indignation is that older children can continue to entertain it by re-evoking the circumstances, while babies abandon it completely.

Equity is a judgment of the individual that people respect the obvious components of a situation. It is equitable for mom to give more food to dad than to the younger children. If she gives more of what one likes to another sibling, it is iniquitous and calls for indignation. What the aggrieved child calls obvious in these situations is synonymous with what he perceives even when this is invisible to everybody else.

On the basis of this changing ground, boys and girls live in a perfectly stable world. So long as they are guided by their perception that what is compatible with the needs of their vital functionings must be offered to them, they cannot perceive contradictions in their demands. They at once know how to turn an argument so that it looks like a perfect justification for their stand. "He started it" is one justification, "She took more than I did" is another; "I warned you" is a third; "I tasted it and I don't like it" is one more.

Children don't have to dwell at length on moral issues, for they live in the moment, and their consciousness remains with the present situation. In the conflicts between their selfish egos, children learn not so much to compromise but to find out how and when they can get all of "it," or if they must leave some for others. Their idea of what is equitable gains flexibility, and they become aware that it is advantageous to yield here and there in order to serve their self-interest better. But life does not demand of them that the responses to specific challenges become principles, or that an overall view of men's motives and their behavior must be found. On the contrary, children demonstrate a very remote and abstract interest in regulating the world.

Anyone who has attempted to give children a role in school or camp government knows that in the assembly empowered to formulate the rules and regulations children are perfectionists. They want the most rigid organization framed with stiff punishments for any breach of the laws. This abstract exercise is done with all seriousness but without much realism. It proves that they are endowed as intellects, containing all that is needed to link cause and effect, to respect internal coherence and to acknowledge premises. It also proves that, as people, they leave the ground of experience and reality to endow their ideas with form but not content.

When they find their laws restrictive and oppressive, they walk out of them as they do from their games. But they feel neither guilty nor rebellious. They are using the logic of action, and if they can get away from the grip of their promises, it is a sign that the logic of action has been fulfilled. They have not yet developed loyalty to abstract coherent systems, and life commands them to break the restrictions on their actions. Actions are the higher court that passes ultimate judgment on what is sensible and acceptable and on what must be rejected as unconstitutional.

17 Equity and Morality: The Ethic of Action

There are issues for which the awarenesses of children are sufficient to produce ethical behaviors. There are others that can confuse a child but offer a point of entry, allowing the child to sort them out after experimentation and reflection. And there are issues where he has neither entry nor interest, and for these utter confusion and even despair are the only adequate forms or response.

Empirically, we all live next to each other, some of us more capable than others of putting up with pressures and rationalizing the behaviors of those who at the same time say they love us but who only want us to be different from what we are. Empirically, we manage to survive mainly because the resilience of the self finds spaces, and even universes, where we are left alone because no one around seems interested in dwelling in them.

Boys and girls, much more than adolescents and adults, prove this resilience by being impervious to moral teaching and by taking on only some of the forms in order to get adults off their backs. By engulfing themselves in actions capable of cutting them off from the rest of the world, they find activities, day after day, that no longer interest adults, that look harmless, and that are perfect vehicles for their dual purpose of being themselves and not being influenced by others.

Boys and girls are moral beings who own an ethic that guides their actions when other people are involved but that is of little account when they are on their own. When they look at themselves in the world, they know that what is most important is their vital education and the ethic tells them to give it their greatest attention, for from their activities a whole person will emerge with criteria and sure sight, a person one can count on, who knows how to live in the universe of action with confidence and equanimity.

That such a confident person looks with a kind of indifference on the sermons that parents shower on him should not surprise us. Many of the adult's words are still empty of meaning and are so passionately delivered that confusion results, although it is not necessarily perceived as one's own confusion. Perhaps, a child may think, it is the state of one who does not know as well as I do that the facts speak for themselves.

The fullness of life that boys and girls enjoy serves as a much more reliable testimony that they are right in their ethical behaviors than do the endlessly repeated "shoulds" and "don'ts" uttered by their elders, which do not apply to the behaviors as they are known from inside. That wrong, and even harm or evil, may result from actions will become understandable to the expert in action that each elementary school child is, when the child is confronted with a genuine situation in which actions and words are the vehicle for comprehension.

18 Interest and Lack of Interest

It is an old adage among elementary school teachers that boys and girls reach their schools keen and enthusiastic and that two years later many of them have dropped out and are present only in body. Many teachers all over the world are at a loss to provide children of this age with meaningful activities. It is no wonder, then, that such innovative proposals as open education, the Nuffield Mathematics Project, the EDC science project, and so on, have been produced to rescue students in schools.

These and other projects suggest that as long as students have some <u>activity</u> to absorb, they will enjoy school, and that from these activities they will gain some academic knowledge valued by adults. This guiding principle confirms that observers have noted the dedication of children to action and have wanted both to nourish it and to use it in their manipulation of school children to make them cover a certain curriculum.

Since boys like to fiddle with anything electrical, a kit can be given them which asks them to use the items that ring a bell when put together correctly.

Part II
Of Boys and Girls

Since boys and girls like to play with water, with sand, with clay, there must be corners in the school, or even each classroom, where children can find these materials and play with them.

Since boys and girls enjoy making noises, a separate space should be provided where they can beat drums or cymbals or other percussion instruments.

Since they like to paint, there should be easels and paints and freedom to produce their pictures. Since they like to draw, desks should be provided which will also be useful for those who discover writing and enjoy it.

The whole organization is made to subordinate school activities to the spontaneous interests shown by students and noted by their teachers. A great step has been taken by those who now offer an education that does not require that children use themselves as adults do. This education is inspired by the analysis of the development of the cognitive powers of children as exemplified in Piaget's work.

So many educators are at the present time fascinated by these two approaches, the first, based on the interests of children, the second, on the lack of interest, that it is appropriate that we devote a few pages to these subjects.

Children are moved to be interested in exactly the same way as adults. The difference lies in what mobilizes the self in each. For boys and girls of elementary school age, it is the universe of action; for adults today, it may be social and political matters, economic or environmental advantages. Everyone, whatever his age, has to become more himself in order to gather the fruits of his dedication to what matters most to him. Boys and girls show an interest in what is accessible in the immanent and a lack of interest in the inaccessible transcendental. So do adults.

Those who say that activity *per se* motivates elementary school children neglect the direction of the overall growth of each child. Those who take the Piagetian view, that some things are outside the interests of children, impose a ceiling on them. Both proposals miss the dynamics of growth and the fact that the co-presence of individuals at different stages in their evolution is capable of creating a contagion which helps each to become more himself.

The study of games in streets and playgrounds clearly indicates that growth is directed by temporal hierarchies generated by the simultaneous presence of definite tasks and of people who are at various stations on their way to mastery. While we must be moved from inside in order to perform, relating what we do to what we have already done, we can find an entry into what we have not yet done only if we perceive that someone in front of us is doing it (except in those few cases when we plunge into a task because it conveys to us that it is possible).

Once we have found a way in, our interest at once feeds back to us whether we should remain or quit. Hence, educators can use interest as an external indicator that the task is proper for that age and stage, but cannot say *a priori* that if we turn our back on the task we lack interest in it. The conclusion can only be that we have either not found an entry into it or that no one has offered us a way in.

Traditional teaching is based on the premise that verbal transactions can replace activity, even prior to active exploration, simply because man has managed to save himself much time and energy by inventing language. This premise is false only in that it offers language before action; only when meanings are offered to support words can language become a vehicle of communication. Piaget and others have called for activity to precede verbalization and put that error right, but they have stopped there, not realizing that activity too can be idle if it is not integrated from within in the larger scheme of individual growth and with the help of contagion and inspiration.

Children clearly stratify the world so that some aspects of it evoke their interest while others leave them indifferent. But if we know how to provide means that displace the boundaries, we leave intact the fact that (for each of us) some things are transcendental at all stages and levels. The presence of the transcendental is the ultimate lever of growth for all of us taken together.

19 Before Adolescence:
On the Threshold of a New World

In the previous chapters we lumped together five years of our lives and only concerned ourselves with the activity we were studying — the shift from contact with change to mastery of it. This was the functional meaning of the age that needed stressing.

While boys and girls will soon shoot up and gain in volume, in weight, and in a greater storage for energy, they have during those years controlled their growth to permit them to work on the fine functionings of the soma as it engages in the various actions that Man has been able to devise over the generations.

As we approach adolescence — which for me is the period of our life when we devote ourselves to the study of our inner dynamics, to affectivity — our interests will show some shifts that are not visible at the beginning of the period we are examining now. In this chapter we shall concentrate on the announcement of the arrival of adolescence and what it does to boys and girls.

The universe of action does not close down at adolescence, and adult life is filled with it. Sports, games, TV shows, all prove that it remains part of life, but the involvement of consciousness differs radically. For boys and girls, action is the fabric of the universe; afterwards it becomes the support for designs and materials that fill action with something else.

We saw in previous chapters that some games with a temporary attraction are coupled with some other activity. A player of marbles can buy, sell, or exchange marbles. This has nothing to do with the game but is a way of seizing an opportunity offered by the social framework available to the players. Another example is the opportunity to try oneself in the role of a leader or a follower in games that involve competing teams.

Most games have a background of other people and social intercourse and offer opportunities to engage in something besides the main definition and purpose of the games. Thus, adults may stress such purposes as monetary gain or prestige or the chance to meet influential people, when they take up card games, or emphasize a professional status when involved in national or international games (some of the latter serving political ends).

For most boys and girls, these opportunities are less perceptible and less attractive, even though from time to time someone draws their attention to the advantage of stressing the discovered opportunity and pursuing it systematically to a notable success in adulthood. Very few boys and girls, for instance, see practicing a musical instrument as an action that might make them concert artists if they pursue it, even when they feel attracted to exploring the possibilities of making sounds with a certain know-how. Very few boys and girls become celebrated acrobats although almost all are fascinated by the exercises and attempt to enter them. They do not know their present flexibility as a wealth to preserve, only as a gift to use for self-knowledge.

Indeed, self-knowledge appears more constantly as a motivation of man's functioning than any other, for it would otherwise be difficult to understand the simultaneous possibility of total involvement in, and of dropping out of, the same activity. It is also self-knowledge that acknowledges the appearance in one's life of a new universe with a kind of command from above that one must explore it.

If boys and girls appear cruel to observers when they submit some animals to torture (to know if they can remain indifferent in the presence of other people's misfortunes), if they hold no grudge over temporary mistreatment of beatings, if they fight savagely and soon afterwards act as friends to their opponents — all this tells us that children of this age have only a marginal entry into the world of feeling that will become their main concern in adolescence. The stress being on action, feelings are less compelling.

Nonetheless, there is always a certain amount of contact with feeling before adolescence. The self creates its sensitivities and perceives what is forced upon it. But the key involvement is in subordinating all that comes from life to the requirement that the self link itself functionally to the outer world by creating all the instruments that lead to the domination of the world. Social elements are judged favorably or unfavorably according to whether they cooperate with one's project or not. A divorce in the family can be more or less traumatic according to whether it reduces or enhances one's chance of pursuing one's own life. A removal to another town likewise. Social events are not seen as social, with their own particular dynamics; they are nuisances, or not much of anything, unless they affect one's life, through reflection or the cultivation of existing sensitivities.

We can therefore look at both sides of the boundary of adolescence and define the areas before and after the threshold: the first is the one in which the need to know the world of action is still predominant, touched perhaps with hints that feelings are winking at the self and encouraging flirtation with them; the second is the one in which the world of action is less dominant and feelings definitely solicit one's awareness.

"Less dominant" does not mean more than it says: still dominant but leaving room for other involvements that can encroach on it. This was unthinkable, not even permitted, earlier.

Action seems to stress the outside world, but in fact it cannot exist without the self and its inner workings. So we are

19 Before Adolescence: On the Threshold of a New World

concerned here with inner shifts, inner dynamics, movements of awareness. Stressing action is the climate of the early years of the age we are looking at; stressing the awareness that the universe of action, as one has become involved in it, has yielded most of what can be perceived and has led to a satisfactory education in terms of finesse, range, and variety, is the climate of the later years. Young people no longer experience their lives as the flow of events and their aftermaths. Time is now studded with one's noticing oneself engaged in events and their sequels.

Boys and girls now notice that action, which once contained all possibilities, can be felt to lack some. The breach is an assessment that a light from beyond action has reached them and also a feeling of satisfaction that they have done most of what was possible to themselves in the prevailing circumstances. Feelings and emotions of all kinds have been experienced from the time of birth or a little after, but they rarely became the center of the self's preoccupation. They were gladly put aside if they prevented the continuation of the exploration of actions. Since the latter has reached a level of satisfaction and feelings continue to be available, the self can pay attention to them. Rather than let them take second place, it can now entertain them, enhance them by its presence, and find that they have a reality of their own that deserves study.

Emotions are existential phenomena. They represent momentary coagulations of energy that cope with a perception and maintain the self in contact with it. They can be dissolved when the contact is no longer necessary, and the energy can be recuperated for future use. The departing energy leaves a "track" in the brain that corresponds to a quality recognizable _per se_ beyond the quantity which it accompanied. It is the quality of the emotion that persist after the emotion itself is dissolved that permits the self to classify emotions and to form a new category in the functionings of the self that we call feelings.

The self involved in living through action learned to favor virtuality for its ease and accuracy; it will do the same during adolescence. It will deliberately shift from emotions to feelings by enhancing emotions and drawing out the dynamics of feeling from them. For this to happen an <u>a priori</u> shift from action to affectivity is required. Although action and affectivity differ by perceptible components, the self recognizes that virtuality is the way of working that increases yield, that speeds up spiritual growth, that makes the boy or girl explore the next layer of life. Actions are now less numerous, and the examination of what they mean to oneself more frequent. In the beginning the world of action still provides the material for brooding, for affective reflection, but the total gift of oneself to action is now missing.

Clearly, as the self intuits the opening up of a new world, it triggers an interest in being more and more involved in this expression of the self. Since, again, this can take place largely without assistance from the outside world, a new phase in the life of the individual announces itself. Although the momentum of the previous activities continues and appearances indicate a still dominant continuity in the expressions of the self, the truth is that an irreversible trend has been launched.

Boys and girls will meet new challenges within. They will feel that they differ more from each other than they thought and will

19 Before Adolescence: On the Threshold of a New World

begin to stress the differences instead of the similarities. They will start thinking of themselves as boys or girls and being proud of their particularities, their distinctive games and occupations. They will begin to cultivate what it means to belong to a particular sex. From being a superficial distinction, sex will gain greater and greater significance.

Inner discoveries will find echoes in the environment and slowly make one recognize that perhaps someone else is going through the same transformations and experiencing the same resonances in the soma. Instead of looking for playmates, one now looks for a friend and investigates friendship.

All this has its beginnings in the later stages of the worship of action, and for many children represents the threshold of the trend that will put actions in the realm of the automatic to make room for the new rules of adolescence. Two years later these rules will have made one forget that not so long ago one belonged to another religion, to a caste and brotherhood dedicated to the rites and rituals of action.

As the earth goes round, the self moves from mastery to mastery to know itself in its place in the world to the extent its gifts permit.

Boys and girls will soon know what it is to be young men and young women in front of new worlds to integrate.

Part III
Spotlights on Adolescence

Introduction:
What is Adolescence?

The domain of adolescence is the domain of feeling, of the inner life. Adolescence is the time when we yield to the call of the inner life. How we yield, how we deal with our feelings, which now come to fill our awareness, serves to integrate the past and open the way to the future. How we use the opportunities offered us in adolescence will importantly determine the quality of our later life, which may be rich or stagnant as a consequence.

Of course, in our perceptions and actions, we are always involved in our inner life. For example, as babies and young children we may know a great deal about where to concentrate, where to put our attention, and how to extract the lessons of where we put ourselves. All this is the work of the inner life. But as babies and young children we do not become absorbed with the workings of this inner life. Our attention is essentially on mastering skills that connect us to the world outside us. In adolescence, our relationship to our inner life becomes the object of our attention. And when this happens, we come upon the challenge of our identity. Each of us asks ourself, "Who am I?" To explore this question, we must turn within ourselves. This is the task of adolescence.

Now, to understand the dynamics of adolescence one must allow for the existence of a component of the self that is best called affectivity. Affectivity, to oversimplify, is feeling. More correctly, it is that component of the self out of which feelings and emotions arise. Affectivity, from another light, is the dynamics of the inner life. How feelings arise, how they can come to fill our beings, how they can disappear only to be replaced by another feeling — all this is part of affectivity and part of the domain of adolescence. Affectivity is also the aspect of the self that takes us into the future. As babies, as children, as adolescents, we regularly face the unknown. What would induce any of us to move into the unknown if we did not have a desire to meet it? That desire is part of affectivity. Without it we would all be paralyzed before the new. Indeed, for those who do not complete the work of adolescence adequately, the new and the unknown can come to seem more and more frightening.

In our childhood, we live action; in our adolescence, we live feeling. Adolescence is the contact of the self with itself. Adolescence is nothing if not the recasting of experience so that the will can express itself more truly in the rest of one's life.

It is that period of life when the self recognizes itself as energy. It sees that it is more than just its behaviors and the process by which it brings these behaviors into being. It sees itself as a participant in a dynamic energetic universe.

Introduction:
What is Adolescence?

To recognize oneself as energy is to become aware of what is in us other than objectifications. This new awareness is precisely what occurs in the adolescent activity of revising the content of one's "soul." While in the preceding period every child only objectified his means of action, now the individual examines his actions with regard to their energy content. In this change we see the fundamental difference separating the general behavior of the boy or girl from that of the young man or young woman, a difference that is immediately visible to all.

The adolescent's search for solitude and his increased sensitivity to pain, whether physical or mental, emphasizes this difference. Memory becomes a much more active and conscious function; this happens because it is concerned with affectivity and the inner life.

In the following pages, we shall describe briefly the adolescent's discovery of friendship and shall try to explain two additional important phenomena in the life of the adolescent — the discovery of religion and thought.

20 The Discovery of Friendship

At adolescence, the contact with energy takes precedence over all else. No longer having to concentrate on the creation of action patterns which are now available and tested, we can take a most immediate step, delayed until now by necessity: we can feel ourselves continuously and not only incidentally as before.

We do not yet know enough of what we are to modify our feelings towards our relatives. Our feelings will only be revised as we discover what makes us human. This discovery is not intellectual, it is direct knowledge of ourselves as energy. Often a painful discovery, it is so profoundly overwhelming that it transforms our whole life. To re-establish our confidence, we project ourselves onto someone else who is living the same experience. In short, we choose a friend, in general from our own environment but outside the family. We create links with our new self — but through the friend. This is why we do not become moralists. Since we do not yet know the qualities of energy, we shall discover them in the other one, as he will in us.

We shall love someone for his own sake. We shall learn to project onto him our ideal; we shall learn to adorn him with the powers we discover to be potential in the energy that animates us and cannot yet analyze. In objectifying these powers we get a better hold on them. In attributing them to someone, we prove the existence of energy. In perceiving its presence in the friend we reach the truth with regard to it.

Thus, the egocentric love of the child matures into friendship. As children, we know only how to receive and did not know the meaning of the act of giving, although this word was used by those who said they were giving to us. Now there is no need to go outside ourselves in order to understand it, no further need for an act of the imagination. We can experience it within. The free nature of the gift is its new merit, its spontaneity, its authenticity.

We experience in ourselves what our egocentrism prevented us from feeling: we become conscious of the creation of affective links, of the creation in ourselves of a place for someone else, of establishing in our affectivity a new living image of the one whom we have chosen to keep in our heart. This friend will live in us, of us.

Someone separate is thus integrated, and has the freedom of moving within us, to be himself and yet intimately ours. This harmony, this new love, is friendship.

With the friend it is not the past which counts, there is none; it is the projection into the future, it is the temporal adventure, lived together, far from those who have a "right" to us and our affections. It is the conquest, we know not of what, but the concerted, accepted conquest, the spiritual conquest first and foremost — of love, of God, of the whole future. The friend is distinct from the parents because with him we leave the realm of the objectified, the known, the established. We undertake the possible and the impossible (we do not yet distinguish them), the unknown, the revolutionary, the new. The friend is the witness of the changes which we hide from all, and, in giving ourselves in all confidence, we know that we run no danger since he surrenders as much of himself to us and we experience each other as if we were a single being.

21 The Discovery of Religion

Each child finds "natural" and "social" elements mixed in his environment. The discovery that there are two worlds, the world of nature and the world of men, is a very slow and sometimes painful process. This discovery becomes possible only for someone at the threshold of self-awareness, when self-awareness isolates him from the rest of creation and when, on the other hand, friendship secures him against loneliness. The two experiences, that there is a self and there is a world, occur at adolescence as spiritual experiences.

In this new awareness, one recognizes oneself as energy and objectification at the same time. But while the objectification aspect is very familiar, the energy aspect is entirely new, and this contact with something new amid the familiar results in a feeling of duality which at the outset is very disturbing. The manifestation of the unknown amid the familiar pulls us up short, leads us to enter more deeply into contact with ourselves, and makes us confer directly with our affectivity — and to ask affective questions to which there are only affective answers. The answers will become objective in the friend who goes through the same experience. But neither we nor our friend has a reply other than that of affectivity, which becomes more and more manifest as questioning becomes more precise, more "educated." Life becomes an affective life. We discover that we are more than we appear to be. In a word, we are feeling.

Affectivity, getting more attention from the self, begins to be organized within it. From its objectifications, the self abstracts any excess energy. This recuperated energy plus the energy accessible in affectivity itself can now be used directly, and it animates the whole energetic universe that is encountered in the heretofore unseen process of objectification.

In particular, the self finds a new inspiration in the rituals of the immediate environment. The adolescent discovers not God but the god of his religion — that is, the god of the symbolism that he has invested in his objectifications. This symbolism comes from his immediate environment, of course; sometimes, it is the symbolism of a formal religion, sometimes it is not. The adolescent understandably has not questioned such objectifications during the former period of his life because he was completely absorbed by the task of creating for himself the frameworks of action.

The discovery of religion is nothing less than the discovery of energy but in the only form that it can take in the adolescent, who can analyze only his own objectifications: the religion of his environment. But this energy is still discovered as a spiritual life because we abundantly clothe it with spirituality. The objectifications of the adolescent gather new truth. They become

21 The Discovery of Religion

a true source of inspiration because they are now spiritualized — and the adolescent is ready to give them the power that symbolism has placed in them.

Thus we discover the god of a religion (if the religion of the environment possesses one), and at the same time, discover the whole of our religion. We feel that all those who belong to it are brothers, and we find, in the saints and the officiating priests, inspirational Masters and Elder Brothers who are capable of acting on our energy through the symbolism of the religion and who lead us still nearer to the heart of the religion. We find that the only path which will lead us to become growing spiritual beings is the path that the symbolism of our religion offers us. The more we discover our spirituality, the more we are caught up in symbolism, which then acquires such an absolute character that we are led to identify spirituality and religious experience within the framework of our particular religious symbolism.

Everywhere the adolescent is the victim of this spiritual mechanism whereby he identifies religion and spirituality. When religion is lacking (because the parents are atheists or the environment has excluded it), the adolescent makes it reappear by allowing himself to be converted or by proposing his own atheism as an absolute, or by using any political or other belief — art for art's sake, art for the people, the pursuit of self-expression, whatever — which is offered him with sufficient conviction.

It is first in himself that the adolescent discovers religion because he discovers there his own essential energy. He then considers <u>the</u> religion the one that his environment offers him. We can say, therefore, that all men are religious, because it is their destiny to recognize themselves as energy at the end of their period of living action and objectification. They do not all belong to a single religion, although each adolescent goes through the same experience, because man objectifies amid a given spiritual symbolism and many religions have been propounded in the world.

If contact with energy is direct and total, it may happen that the adolescent transcends one symbolism and discovers another, but this is so rare that the phenomenon can be referred to only as a theoretical possibility. Cases of spontaneous conversion from one religion to another do exist. Saint Paul more or less symbolizes this case, Uriel da Costa realized it.

22 The Discovery of Thought

At the same time as the adolescent discovers religion, he is organizing his affectivity. This means that he is consciously building affective categories for himself.

In his solitude, he is able to experience all degrees of sorrow, joy, pleasure, nervous exhaustion, exaltation, tension. He recognizes similarities and nuances, and he forms a profoundly <u>felt</u> classification which serves as a basis for recognizing the experiences in the future. In other words, emotions are experienced analytically, and feelings are identified as frameworks for these emotions. Feelings thus come to form affective categories.

Becoming aware of a feeling and of the emotions which compose it is not like becoming aware of an objectification. An objectification is organized, statified energy. A feeling, in contrast, is not organized energy but energy <u>itself</u> in a characteristic state of tension. Recognizing a feeling is recognizing a particular state of energy. The experience of anger or rage, of pleasure or happiness, available to all of us, is a clear example. The formation of feelings is possible at adolescence because this is the period of life when contact with energy takes place.

In adolescence, feelings are consciously created, and they constitute a framework not only for affective and moral life, but also — and this is a critical point — for intellectual life.

As adolescents discover their religion in their energy, they discover Thought (the thought of their time) in their language, with the categories of feelings serving as frameworks for the known but not yet fully understood experiences. At this point the adolescent freely thinks his own thoughts. He has, for the first time, an intellectual logic which codifies the mechanism of action — until now, he has only lived action and not been aware of it or of the motivating force of affective energy behind it — a mechanism that is rendered real through the categories of feelings. Action and affectivity (with its dynamics) give birth to thought per se. Thought is dynamic, because it is active, and it integrates all the possibilities of action experienced so far plus the possibilities that the freedom of the self give it.

It is because energy reaches itself that thought can became aware of itself and be recognized as true independently from logic, which thought proves rather than the reverse. Logic is the mechanism of thinking; it adds nothing to intellectual life, it only defines one of its aspects.

Intellectual life is energetic life — because it derives from affectivity and because it represents a new possibility for itself, that of recognizing itself in the reorganization of action brought about by the categories of feelings. In thought, a new type of structure is created which is no longer the direct objectification of energy — as is action — but rather a structure of abstraction. The self, which discarded its objectifications in order to know the emotions and recognize in them feelings, pursues in its affective analysis an operation that extracts what is similar and dissimilar. From these extractions comes the new structure, which is thought. There is no break between the conceptual formation of feelings (which come from the classification of emotions) and intellectual classifications (which come from the classification of objectifications).

Although thought exists all through life, it is a discovery of adolescence because thought then becomes aware of itself. This discovery is a genuinely new awareness. The stuff to be made explicit exists already in the form of energy in both affectivity and objectifications, but the sensitivity to this energy generates an awareness that one is directly associated with an aspect of the self not yet studied. The adolescent undergoes the new experience that one can individually direct one's thought and can genuinely assert what is happening within oneself. This is the reason assertion is a characteristic behavior during adolescence.

Since the impact of this material on one's consciousness results from recuperated energy and the re-examination of previous objectifications, one has both a solid sense of reality and a feeling of the unformed, the labile. From the first a cockish certainty may result, from the second a sense of weakness and an uncertainty about the content of one's awareness. This explains why it is not possible to have a set of responses which are firm enough to lead us to a standard classification of what adolescents think in most matters. No longer exclusively engaged in action, they see more than what they had perceived in actions and situations. But they are not yet certain of what they perceive in a field they have not sufficiently articulated to themselves.

The logic of action gives way before thought. Thought is the perception of a fleeting new sensitivity to what accompanies emotional upheavals: one can now assert that some things are happening to oneself which were not happening before. Since upheavals are determinedly pursued by the adolescents as being the true stuff of awareness — they live within these upheavals — there is no possibility for them to account for the upheavals through the logic of action, which uses given actions to achieve given ends. A new logic has to be developed. The time it takes varies with individuals and may even cover several few years. But when it is formed it is a logic aware of itself, <u>intellectual logic</u>.

This new logic permits lengthy verbalized arguments, which are stained by the organized categories covering all one has gone through: the childhood objectifications that involve perceptions and actions; the stabilization of the energy flow between the newly examined objectifications; and the immediate gathering of experienced data made available by the total re-examination of the content of the self and the settlement of the main issues raised during this hyperactive period.

Still, thought is more than intellectual logic, for the latter is the form of thought designed for social intercourse, and thought itself is capable of transcending experience, present and past. It can find uncharted fields in the accumulated stuff that fills the mind. Because it can transcend experience, it is free. It can give a new life, a unique tint, to one's total experience. Thought can become a source of new statements about what goes on in one's intellect as the intellect becomes aware of some content that so far had been unnoticed or of some unrecognized relations between awareness or of some dynamics until then taken for granted. This is intellectual creation. The set of such discoveries goes to form the intellectual material by which one helps create oneself, some of it may even remain in the culture of one or more groups.

It does not seem possible for the adolescent to think outside of the intellectual frameworks of the environment, but thought may seize all the truth that these intellectual frameworks contain. The awareness that what they contain is true, that the content of language and abstract knowledge (as signs of the creativity of the mind) are absolutely justified, is an event of adolescence, and characterizes adolescence as much as does the growth of awareness through religion. At this point in the individual's intellectual development, it is not logic that justifies the intellect and its products. Now it is the direct knowledge of the free intellect, which brings us to the examination of categories and forces us to construct a logic for ourselves.

Insofar as it is distinguished from logic, thought is a spiritual, human function — that is, an expression of the self in its freedom. The adolescent gives us the proof of this freedom every day, by his refusal to think logically, by his lack of appreciation of logical constructions in the rational sciences, and by the use that he makes of contradiction to discover himself as energy. He creates no confusion in himself from the fact that some of his propositions are self-contradictory, and he can be perfectly loyal to two opposed ideas when they are set out for him. This is an everyday experience for all those who live with adolescents.

Since the adolescent discovers thought, it seems appropriate to offer a brief comment on the lessons for education that follow from our discussion.

Intellectual education should follow the true inner life of the adolescent and take into account the psychological sequences we have examined. In this way, we shall spare our young boys and girls much time and many frustrations. If we want a strong and well-equipped intellect, we must first create the conditions that allow the awareness of thought as a spiritual function — an awareness of the freedom of thought, of its creative power, of its discriminating use of states of energy and objectifications. Once we do this, the proper function of thought in life will be exercised with vigor and, indeed, without external pressure.

Thought will not necessarily take the form of rediscovering an existing system of thought, as Piaget would have it. Rather, its form is likely to resemble the discovery of religion: a discovery within the framework of the intellectual environment, but a discovery that also contains the ability of going beyond. Realizing thought in this form will place our students in a relation to the future, with an expectation of and a respect for its originality.

By its handling of the education of the adolescent, today's intellectually oriented society has established the lie that the human hierarchy stops at intellectual mastery. It cultivates only the intellectual scaffolding, ignoring altogether the soul of thought: dynamic affectivity. Fortunately — for all of us — the adolescent often brings to bear his own experience.

23 The Adolescent and Love

I have argued that adolescence should be defined as an inner, spiritual experience not as a physiological state. We have just examined how thought, far from being alien to affectivity, arises out of it. I believe there is another perspective which needs to be reversed in order to understand the adolescent. It is the theory concerning the connection between puberty and love.

It is widely accepted that adolescence and sexual interest are intimately intertwined, and that puberty, which makes reproduction possible, and sexuality, are, in effect, two aspects of the same phenomenon.

Indeed, certain authors have defined adolescence by the onset of puberty. But the fact is that the sex hormones of puberty are liberated very late and that the principal roles in their release is played by the pituitary, a tissue which is half brain and half gland. Puberty is therefore under the control of the brain, and its arrival seems to wait on something. What is it that will decide this tremendous liberation which will alter such a large number of functions and make the child almost adult from the psychic point of view? Is it not likely that the human being becomes capable of loving not because he is pubescent but becomes pubescent because he is capable of love?

When the child, who has created his frameworks of action, discovers himself as inner energy, his power of loving appears to him for the first time. He discovers "the other" as a spiritual being and this discovery will shift the emphasis of his life, so that it is lived under quite new conditions. We have seen how the adolescent re-examines affectively his relationship with all his objectifications, how he orients himself towards the creation of his own thought and his faith.

From the somatic point of view, he also takes stock of himself. He already knows how to use himself efficiently in all his actions, but his field of action will now be widened. He will realize his maximum possibility by bringing to action his maximum potential energy: in growing. While small muscles are necessary to control action, large ones are needed to realize it to the full, and puberty is a period of rapid somatic growth. In the field of action, the adolescent places all the emphasis on power rather than on precision and speed. This new power suggests to the adolescent that he is a physical energy; the adolescent builds on this framework of feelings.

The same physiological mechanism produces both somatic and glandular growth. As a result of this growth, there appears a being ready to live a complete life, including sexual love and reproduction (which are not essential human forms but express human possibilities). Puberty is the somatic echo of the attainment of energy. Power is felt physically, intellectually, psychically, socially.

It is not by chance that Nietzsche and Schopenhauer have had so much success with adolescents, nor that the psychology of Adler has so many disciples among them. An adolescent quickly understands and adopts the notion of "inferiority complex." We are roused by this concept because the true idea behind it is that of power, the feeling of which we all experience in our adolescence.

Puberty and marriageability are connected only because in ancient civilizations puberty was an obvious indication of power. Today, puberty and the age for marriage are no longer synonymous. Procreation does not bestow the right to take a spouse; economic conditions must also be favorable. Puberty is no longer a sign of social power. It is one somatic aspect of a certain moment in life when many things are demanded of an individual.

Puberty itself no longer gives the right to complete love. It does, of course, allow the sex act, which society today confuses with love. But when the adolescent experiences love, he himself does not give pre-eminence to the sex act as adults do. For him, love is spiritual and the sex act animal. He will perpetrate it, if necessary, but he will rarely find his happiness in it. He will study it, dispassionately, will know it as an external act, but he will not regard it as the image of love.

These comments may sound terribly naive and as if written by someone from another planet. Yet there is plenty of evidence gathered from adolescent diaries and psychologists' reports to justify the statements about the priority of love among young men and women who may have also indulged, when not in love, in all sorts of sexual practices. Since adolescence is so short compared with the whole of life, the preoccupation with pure love during this period may look insignificant as compared with the visible interest in sex symbols and sexual objects. But it is not clock time that should occupy us. What matters, rather, is the intensity of experiencing, and in adolescence we discover about love what will be our wealth for the rest of our life.

The separation of love and sexuality may have terrible consequences for a sensitive youth, torn between his beliefs and those of the environment. For him, love is much more beautiful if pure. It is not love if it be not pure. Many adults believe that the disturbances of youth arise because the adolescent does not exercise his sexual function. The anguish which so many adolescents experience in their contact with sexual behavior is the source of much graver conflicts than the presumed ones of abstinence. The adolescent, to prove to himself that he is normal, assumes an attitude in which love is but a sexual game. He loses his most precious conquest, his spirituality, and is thrown back on objectifications as such.

The sexual art of loving which excites the curiosity of the adolescent leaves him profoundly skeptical. Fortunately, when he discovers love, he recognizes it immediately and desperately wants to preserve it from being sullied.

In all climates the songs of love are similar, and the male student who sings parodies would never do so before a woman who moves him. For the adolescent, love is spiritual and love is pure because he has transcended the physiological in his adolescent experience.

Further Readings

1. C. Gattegno, <u>What We Owe Children</u>, New York City, 1970

2. C. Gattegno, <u>Towards a Visual Culture</u>, New York City, 1969

3. C. Gattegno, <u>The Generation of Wealth</u>, New York City, 1986

4. C. Gattegno, <u>The Science of Education, Part 1: Theoretical Considerations</u>, New York City, 1987

All these publications are available from: Educational Solutions, www.EducationalSolutions.com

www.ingramcontent.com/pod-product-compliance
Lightning Source LLC
Chambersburg PA
CBHW080539170426
43195CB00016B/2612